TORONTO THE GOOD?

Negotiating Race in the Diverse City

Armed with the motto "Diversity Our Strength," the City of Toronto has garnered a world-class reputation for challenging racism, largely because of how it is seen to value and include racialized groups through its diversity policies and practices. *Toronto the Good?* unsettles popular depictions of both diversity and the City of Toronto by attending to what diversity does in and for the City in the context of historical relations of race.

Toronto the Good? brings together Shana Almeida's critical insights as a former political staff member along with her years of in-depth research on diversity in the City of Toronto to offer a compelling case to rethink how we understand diversity and racial inclusion in the City of Toronto and beyond. Initiated in a local context, *Toronto the Good?* critically contributes to global discussions on diversity, race, democracy, political participation, and power.

SHANA ALMEIDA is an assistant professor in the School of Professional Communication at the Toronto Metropolitan University. Her research and teaching contributions are informed by over six years as a senior political staff member at the City of Toronto.

Toronto the Good?

Negotiating Race in the Diverse City

SHANA ALMEIDA

UNIVERSITY OF TORONTO PRESS
Toronto Buffalo London

ISBN 978-1-4875-0427-4 (cloth)   ISBN 978-1-4875-1981-0 (EPUB)
ISBN 978-1-4875-6053-9 (paper)   ISBN 978-1-4875-1980-3 (PDF)

Library and Archives Canada Cataloguing in Publication

Title: Toronto the good? : negotiating race in the diverse city /
Shana Almeida.
Names: Almeida, Shana, author.
Description: Includes bibliographical references and index.
Identifiers: Canadiana (print) 20220268401 | Canadiana (ebook) 20220268479 |
ISBN 9781487504274 (cloth) | ISBN 9781487560539 (paper) |
ISBN 9781487519803 (PDF) | ISBN 9781487519810 (EPUB)
Subjects: LCSH: Cultural pluralism – Ontario – Toronto. |
LCSH: Toronto (Ont.) – Race relations.
Classification: LCC FC3097.9.A1 A46 2022 | DDC 305.8009713/
541 – dc23

We wish to acknowledge the land on which the University of Toronto Press
operates. This land is the traditional territory of the Wendat, the Anishnaabeg,
the Haudenosaunee, the Métis, and the Mississaugas of the Credit First Nation.

University of Toronto Press acknowledges the financial support of the
Government of Canada, the Canada Council for the Arts, and the Ontario Arts
Council, an agency of the Government of Ontario, for its publishing activities.

Canada Council Conseil des Arts
for the Arts du Canada

ONTARIO ARTS COUNCIL
CONSEIL DES ARTS DE L'ONTARIO

an Ontario government agency
un organisme du gouvernement de l'Ontario

Funded by the   Financé par le
Government   gouvernement
of Canada   du Canada

Canadä

For Olive, who is my greatest love, and my greatest teacher

Contents

Contents

Preface

This book isn't really about diversity. What started as a study of diversity in City of Toronto transformed into a book project that carefully traces the unrelenting and productive dimensions of race; specifically, how race continues through "progressive" discourses like diversity alongside varying modes of racial inclusion, beginning with the multicultural turn of the 1970s. At the heart of this exploration of discourse, race, and the City of Toronto is Stuart Hall's (2021) call:

> We have to uncover for ourselves in our own understanding, as well as for the students we are teaching, the often deep structural factors which have a tendency to persistently not only generate racial practices and structures but reproduce them through time, which account for their extraordinarily immovable character. (p. 126)

Hall brilliantly explains how economic and socio-racial/relational factors work in tandem and are reinforced in the political realm, to continue Britain's explicitly racial character. This is an especially important point, one that is also echoed by this book: *the structural cannot be divorced from the political*. It is in the political realm that race is continuously remade to make sense, and by extension, where structural factors find their footing. We need look no further than the devastating global impacts of the COVID-19 pandemic, particularly for Black, Indigenous, and racialized communities. Perhaps these impacts are discussed or even measured by some governments, including the City of Toronto, but never really in ways that explicitly point to state-led pandemic responses as an exercise in biopolitics, a kind of modern-day racially informed "survival of the fittest." If this pandemic has taught us anything, it is that structural factors are rooted in racial histories that both predate the state and inform its workings.

Hall also warns that race is not a matter of (ill) feelings. As such, race cannot be done away with by inviting or amplifying "good feeling," "gentle reform" (2021, p. 126), good racial deeds, and feel-good discourses such as diversity. In fact, the opposite is true. As this book will show, diversity *keeps race going*. Our collective work is thus to carefully uncover what rests below the surface of diversity and other institutionalized discourses – the ideological conditions that are deeply organizing, penetrative, and unrelenting, across time and space.

In this sense, although set in the City of Toronto, the findings of this book have more far-reaching implications. Diversity moves are becoming increasingly globalized, and with them, a widespread reorganization of discussions on race/racism, especially in institutional spaces like government, organizations (both public and private), and the academy. Understanding the terms of this reorganization is crucial. However, the interventions that this book makes begin with an understanding that diversity thrives in each of our locations across the globe, under specific terms and through specific practices. Following Sara Ahmed (2012), I thus ask that, in our respective locations, we trace how and under what terms diversity discourse also becomes a reorganizing tactic. When we do this work – tracing how and under what specific terms diversity reorganizes race/racism – we can begin to build a global reservoir of critical knowledge and strategies that illuminate and address the enduring effects of race, in and across our spaces.

I have attempted to tackle this work in the context of the City of Toronto. But in the spirit of building collective knowledge and strategies, I might say that this book is not really about the City of Toronto either – at least not exclusively, once we consider the eerie familiarity of the racial tropes I trace and illuminate.

As the late brilliant Black feminist writer, professor, and activist bell hooks (1992) also reminds us, racial Others get consumed in spaces of whiteness. Discussions on interrogating, decentring, and/or abolishing whiteness are mitigated or even deemed irrelevant because the very presence of "diverse" bodies in institutional spaces affords institutions the all-too-familiar "room for all" rhetoric. Put simply, diversity reorganizes race through presence. As I write in the case of the City of Toronto, any critical questioning of diversity becomes difficult when racial Others are invited to the table, and even more so *when they make up the whole table*. What this means, and what we must reckon with is that racial inclusion (alone) is not necessarily a good thing. Of course scholars such as Trinh T. Minh-ha, W.E.B. Du Bois, bell hooks, and others have been warning us about the dangers of racial inclusion in institutional contexts for years now. My hope is that this book adds depth to these claims, by carefully tracing how, why, and under what terms racial inclusion can be complicit in projects of whiteness.

As diversity discourse lives on, we are also witnessing an orchestrated full-on attack on everything (and everyone) in the field of critical race theory (CRT). This has translated into un/de-funded critical projects, denied tenures, hate mail, and the outright silencing of critical, often Black, Indigenous, and racialized voices, alongside the retention and promotion of vitriolic public intellectuals, calls to cancel "cancel culture," and denials of racism, in and outside of the academy. In the academy, many attacks on CRT are justified under the supposedly neutral banners of "academic freedom" and/or "freedom of expression," which, as I have written elsewhere with some of my colleagues (Joseph et al., 2019), are ultimately meant to protect white supremacy. It is worth noting here that I and many of my racialized friends and mentors in the academy are no strangers to the roadblocks when pursuing critical race work, including the denial of funding for our scholarly research and publications. This book project has certainly been no exception. But as my dear friend and colleague Professor Marty Fink wrote to me recently, quoting Sarah Schulman (2021), "When you make a film that is a blueprint for challenging authority and the powers that be ... you can't expect that the powers that be will reward you" (p. xxii).

Whether inside or outside the academy, whether through a film, book, article, research project, classroom space, meeting, community, organization, protest, or revolution, one thing remains clear: that we continue to remain hopeful and fight for change, for justice, is a testament to the resilience of our desire to build for the better.

This – not diversity – is our strength.

Acknowledgments

This book would not have come to fruition without the support and encouragement of my friends, colleagues, and comrades – many of whom share their stories of survival and hold space for my own. We exist in a world where solidarities are dwindling. I am grateful for spaces and friendships that continue to centre community building.

To my dearest friends, who called me at all hours of the day and night to see if I was surviving, if I was eating, if my face had seen the sun, and if I needed anything, thank you for believing in me. Thank you for continuously reminding me to be in the moment, to take each task on, day by day, and to ask for support when I needed it.

My parents struggled with violent experiences of racism when they came to Canada and thereafter. I want to thank them for their courage in the face of sheer adversity and trauma. They inspire a lot of my work. The racism we faced as a family shaped who we were and how we related to one another, for many, many years. We spent a lot of time in pain. Writing this book is part of my healing.

Thank you to Daniel Quinlan, acquisitions editor at University of Toronto Press, for entertaining my countless emails at all hours of the day and night. Your support was invaluable, and this book would not have happened without your guidance.

Thank you to Dr. Karim Murji and Dr. Giovanni Picker, co-editors of the special issue of the *International Journal of Sociology and Social Policy*, for including a small part of this book as a journal article entitled "Mythical Encounters: Challenging Racism in the Diverse City." Thank you also to *Wagadu: A Journal of Transnational Women's and Gender Studies*, who published some of the preliminary ideas and findings of my archival research in "Exposing the Threads: A Critical Interrogation of the Policies, Practices and (Non)Performativity of Diversity in the City of Toronto," for a special issue edited by Dr. Nikita Dhawan and Dr. Sara Ahmed.

I am especially grateful to those who shared their experiences of doing diversity in the City of Toronto. You trusted me to be a witness to the ways of navigating and reflecting on being racialized staff in the City. Our conversations will stay with me for a long time. I am indebted to you for learning (and coming to terms with) just how powerful diversity can be, in the City of Toronto and beyond.

TORONTO THE GOOD?

Negotiating Race in the Diverse City

Chapter One

The Diversification of Diversity

In July 2015 a giant yellow billboard was erected by the side of a main highway in the state of Arkansas, decreeing "Diversity Is Code for White Genocide" (Bowden, 2017).[1] A friend who knew I was research-ing diversity in Toronto's municipal government[2] sent me a link to a photo of the billboard later that year, along with a message explaining how grateful she was that we live in Toronto, a city[3] so wonderfully welcoming to diversity. Of course, the rhetoric that Toronto is *the* diversity haven has been circulating for as long as I can remember. Keil and Kipfer (2003) explain how the myth of Toronto as a colourful mosaic of ethnically diversified, peaceful communities has contributed significantly to sustain-ing Canada's national identity as everything that America is not. Toronto activist and journalist Desmond Cole (2015) also writes, "There's this idea that Toronto is becoming a post-racial city, a multicultural utopia where the colour of your skin has no bearing on your prospects" (para. 11). These myths continue to define, on a global scale, what Toronto is and has always been, despite Toronto being home to the Ku Klux Klan and other white supremacist organizations since the 1970s (Bateman, 2014) and, more recently, the theory that diversity compels "white genocide" (see, e.g., Zhou, 2018; Bogart, 2019).

I became well acquainted with this "diversity haven" narrative in my former life as a political staffer in the City of Toronto, and am now still, as a scholar who gives international talks. My research sought in part to understand how the City of Toronto conveys this sense of place to the world. But when I saw the picture of the billboard, I was also struck by how the term "diversity" could imply a threat in some spaces yet be defined as a feature and asset of others. If diversity could signify white genocide and the inclusion and welcoming of difference,[4] how many other ways diversity could be taken up, for what purposes, and by whom? Crucially, are these ways as different from one another as they might appear? I was also reminded of Himani Bannerji (2000), who compels us to critically explore the banal presence of the term "diversity" in terms of what it does politically. Diversity can shape the way spaces and bodies within those spaces are conceived. The question I had was, How?

This book explores the ways in which diversity shapes, shifts, travels, and encapsulates. Diversity circulates in and across spaces by attaching to "different" bodies. It can be celebrated, anxiety-producing, and threatening. It can authorize acceptance and rejection. In short, diversity does many things. Much like Ahmed (2012) was, I became thoroughly invested in following diversity around, to see what it does and does not do. However, I began the research for this book with the idea that diversity could "do" different things and could be thought of and "done" differently, *depending on where and with/by whom.*

My research on diversity began after years of reflecting on my own work as a former political staffer in the City. I often still think about what diversity did for me, as one of the very few racialized women in a senior political staff position. I learned quickly that I could use the language of diversity to disguise my insertions of an anti-racist agenda in the City's policies and practices. In fact, I became confident that I could gain the support of City Councillors and political and bureaucratic staff for my initiatives because I argued for anti-racist action in diversity terms. I initiated policies calling for the representation of Toronto's "diverse communities" in decision-making, believing that City officials would know exactly what (or more precisely, who) I meant by "diverse communities." Looking back, I cannot recall anyone ever asking for clarification. As a self-proclaimed anti-racist activist, I thought I had spearheaded meaningful, institutional, anti-racist change in the City.

But in whatever ways I may have used it, diversity always ended up being about the same thing: race and racial "difference." I never once considered this, let alone sought to change it. Until a few years ago, I had not thought about how diversity is and continues to be synonymous with race, in the City of Toronto and beyond. As Lentin and Titley (2011) write, "[Diversity] always has a constitutive centre, unquestioned and assumed" (p. 10). This is the most crucial point to consider, in terms of what diversity does: the "smokescreen of diversity" (Darder & Torres, 2004, p. 1) enables a simultaneous synonymity and obscuring of race, which remains largely unexamined and/or unchallenged in everyday writing and speech acts.

Ergo, this book. I wrote this book to make the invisible visible. More specifically, this book introduces theoretical and empirical provocations that seek to expose what undergirds and obscures the co-articulation(s) and reproduction(s) of diversity and race in the City of Toronto. The theories I will present draw on the brilliant works of those who write at the intersections of feminist theory, critical race theory, gender theory, anti-colonial thought, sociology, political theory, cultural theory, and/ or postcolonial theory, to name a few. They also intend to expand on the evocative works of Sara Ahmed and Nirmal Puwar.

Ahmed (2012) explains how diversity work can entail insisting on belonging in institutional spaces where racial Others are not expected and/or assumed to be. The very act of insisting on your belonging can, as Ahmed suggests, confirm "the improper nature of your residence" (p. 177). Puwar (2004) similarly examines what happens when racialized and women's bodies occupy spaces in which they are seen not to belong. Taking up the notion of C.W. Mills's (1997) "somatic norm,"[5] Puwar shows how institutional spaces historically reserved for white men continue to be bound by whiteness and masculinity *as an effect of* the increasing presence of racialized employees, particularly those in senior positions.[6] Through his unmarked body and freedom to move in space, the somatic norm at once confirms and determines – at the very least psychically – that "diverse" Others are trespassers. As bodies "out of place,"[7] painful encounters with white colleagues are additionally fraught with questions of legitimacy. Ahmed (2021) echoes this sentiment: diversity can be about reconfirming who gets to do what, and where racial Others can and cannot go.

Although Ahmed and Puwar make poignant statements about the historical, social, political, and racial constructions of space, belonging, and bodies, Puwar (2004) also suggests that certain elements permit certain Othered bodies to conditionally belong, as "familiar rather than unfamiliar strangers" (p. 123). During my research process, I became intrigued by the intricacies of belonging/not-belonging in space, specifically the terms under which belonging is "granted," felt, and/or denied to racial Others in a City that requires the inclusion of racial difference to make itself up as "diverse." For me, the City of Toronto could not claim to be "one of the most diverse cities in the world [who] has gained an international reputation for the successful management of its diversity" (City of Toronto, 2003a, p. 2) without the inclusion and support of at least *some* racial Others. But as I advance in this book, to discuss inclusion and/or belonging for racial Others in the City and under the terms of diversity as a matter of being a "particular kind" of racial Other can be too simplistic, perhaps even dangerous. I instead conceive of and explore belonging for racial Others in the diverse City of Toronto as a constant *negotiation*. In this vein, I wanted to understand how and why racial Others still negotiate their belonging in the City, if what these negotiations accomplish is simply a reconfirmation and reproduction of race and power in space, as both Ahmed and Puwar suggest. What else might these negotiations of belonging offer, accomplish, and/or do for racial Others in the City? How might diversity enable and/or foreclose these negotiations?

This book addresses these questions. Throughout, it also attends to how diversity is articulated spatially. As Lentin (2011) poignantly describes it, "[D]iversity implies a confined and recognizable space. It is curry and couscous but not hungry and destitute asylum seekers; it is bangles and ankle chains but not hijabs" (p. 120). What we must thus interrogate, drawing on Razack (2002), is how "diverse" space produces bodies, and conversely how bodies produce "diverse" space.

One aim of this book is to show how and under what terms racism is taken up in a City that repeatedly claims and is known for its global leadership in addressing diversity and racism and that governs Toronto – what McDonald and Davey (2016) have named "the most diverse city on earth." Indeed, as a City we appear to have cornered the market on all things "diverse." But what do the spatial confines of the diverse City of Toronto mean for claims of racism within/against it? Many would say that diversity makes speaking about racism difficult if not impossible, in the City of Toronto and beyond. I offer a more nuanced take, one that hopefully also reorients our view of what (or who) we – racial Others in particular – are up against, in the City of Toronto and other spaces organized in diversity terms.

Toronto the Good: Critical Contexts

Much work on diversity has focussed on larger influences that have triggered and/or shaped its particular institutionalization(s). Henry et al. (2017), for example, situate the pursuit of diversity within the neoliberal agenda of the nation state. They draw attention to the global spread of neoliberalism, rooted in the market values and radical individualism of Thatcher/Reagan era and upheld in the 1980s by the Mulroney government in Canada. Mulroney's neoliberal agenda resulted in a shift away from multiple programs, including employment equity and immigration and settlement, as well as a de-funding of many social justice-oriented community organizations. Importantly, the authors argue that a central consequence of these neoliberal shifts in Canada was a turn towards a diversity that is "experienced individually" (p. 13), quantifiable, marketable and competitive. This neoliberal diversity permeates every aspect of institutional life (Henry et al., 2017).

In a similar vein, Good (2009) and Keil (2002) argue that the neoliberal agenda of Ontario's Conservative government, under Premier Mike Harris, had severe impacts on the way Toronto took up diversity, immigration, and racism. Elected in 1995, perhaps the biggest of Harris's "cost-saving measures" was the amalgamation of Toronto's seven local governments into one municipality – the City of Toronto – in 1998. Keil additionally documents how, although generally antagonistic toward anything to do with the City of Toronto's diversity work, the Harris government marketed the megacity's diversity internationally, in the interests of accumulating capital. Importantly, the province's marketing strategy also framed and organized Toronto's racialized and immigrant communities' lobbying of the federal government for local immigration settlement funding, wherein organizers strategically tethered the success of Toronto's "diverse" communities to the City's economic development. This too had an impact on how and why diversity is taken up in the City of Toronto in market terms.

Many scholars also assert that the City of Toronto's diversity policies and practices draw directly from Canada's multiculturalism policies and celebrations of ethnic differences (see, e.g., Boudreau et al., 2009; Catungal & Leslie, 2009; Goonewardena & Kipfer, 2005; Rosa, 2019). But could there be aspects of diversity in the City of Toronto that are *site-specific*? Some scholars take this question up. For example, in his analysis of Toronto's Regent Park public housing redevelopment, Mele (2019) shows how the City of Toronto's urban planning and development policies produce, sustain, and protect a distinctly urban neoliberalism and diversity, aimed at redeeming the urban poor.

I argue that our preoccupation with whose "diversity" affects/shapes who and in what way(s) often detracts us from investigating how diversity moves, shifts, and encapsulates, with and through space. I also heed the call of Jacobs (1996) that we attend to the space of the local, to trace the site-specific processes that incite re-articulations of race and power that also bound the nation and transverse the globe. This book shows how the City's spatially bound diversity claims enable and are regenerated by specific, localized practices that "do" something to and with experiences of racism in the City of Toronto, as well as to and with the bodies that describe them. Initiated locally, this book also invites critical interrogations of diversity in other institutional spaces and the specific, local practices that continue to make it up. As I have written elsewhere (Almeida, 2019), when we understand how diversity and race manifest and coalesce locally, we can begin to develop a global reservoir of strategies that understand and seek to undermine their re-authorizations as they shift, travel, and encapsulate, in and across institutions.

Diversity Our Strength: The Local Context

Armed with its motto "Diversity Our Strength," Toronto's municipal government is lauded by scholars, researchers, organizations, and policymakers for being a world leader in tackling issues related to diversity, inequality, and racism (see, e.g., Averill, 2009; Good, 2009; Graham & Phillips, 2007; Ontario Human Rights Commission, 2010; Qadeer, 2016; Siemiatycki, 2011). In her study comparing the municipal governments of several Canadian cities (which she calls "sub-states"), Tossutti (2012) concludes that the City of Toronto is the only municipal government that fully embraces and embeds diversity in its policies and practices, and as such, prioritizes remedying disadvantage – through racism, human rights, access and equity, and/or immigration – for ethno-racial groups. For these and other scholars, researchers, organizations, and policymakers, the focus has largely been on how to make the City even more inclusive and democratic – as Kymlicka (1995) would say, to accommodate "minority groups demanding recognition of their identity" (p. 10). This literature largely discusses racial inequalities as part of political/state systems-in-flux as they scramble to address increasing racial diversity in cities. The way to address racial inequalities in the City is thus more diversity policies and practices.

Scholars also observe that despite the City's motto and its many policies and practices encouraging diversity and inclusion, racism in the City of Toronto remains pervasive (Ahmadi, 2018; Croucher, 1997; Gross, 2007; Joy & Vogel, 2015; Valverde, 2012). As Boudreau et al. (2009) argue, diversity has become so central to the identity of the City of Toronto that any threat to this harmonious image is silenced. Ahmadi and Tasan-Kok (2013) also write that the City's diversity rhetoric does little to disrupt stereotypes based on race and class, and in fact furthers the stigmatization of poor racialized neighbourhoods at the edges of Toronto.

Importantly, this literature instead hints at *how race underwrites political/state systems*. Goldberg (2002) explains how the centrality of race in the configuration of the state is reflected not only in the racist implications of state policies or the under-representation of racialized bodies in state institutions, but also, perhaps more importantly, through the very (racial) nature in which "accesses and restrictions, inclusions and exclusions, conceptions and modes of representation" (p. 104) are conceived and authorized. In this, states are produced to *uphold, continue, and normalize the validity of race*. This perspective can be challenging to think through, especially when set against "proof" of the increasing participation and inclusion of racial Others in City of Toronto life. This book presents a more nuanced view of racial Others' participation and inclusion, including the racial terms through which both are authorized, which I hope advances our understanding of the centrality of race in the configuration of the City of Toronto as wonderfully "diverse."

Toronto the Good: The Research Project

Anchoring this work is a critical exploration of diversity in the City of Toronto as a discourse, and as a mechanism of power. Stoler (1995) writes that power organizes and reproduces "truths" (or truth-claims) justifying historical, social, and racial distinctions and exclusions in the world, through discourse. But as Hook (2007) also reminds us, discourse must contain its discontinuities, exclusions, and alternative accounts, for its truths to appear as natural and as a "given," across time. This also includes the containment of *racial bodies, psyches, and subjectivities.* Hence my hypothesis: the discursive containment(s) afforded by diversity has implications for racial Others who are "included" in the diverse City, particularly for racialized City staff who are charged with "doing" diversity work.

The research project I pursued thus had two objectives: (1) to unearth and illuminate the discontinuities, exclusions, and alternative accounts of diversity discourse in the City of Toronto; and (2) to explore how diversity discourse, its historical "truths" and effects produce and are reproduced through the subjectivities of racialized City of Toronto staff.

Method

To frame my investigation, I drew on tenets of Michel Foucault's genealogy as a method. Genealogy asks "what is happening now" and how this "now" is a re-emergence of historical relations of power in the present (Tamboukou, 1999). Perhaps the most challenging aspect of this method is the understanding that power radiates everywhere, through speech acts, texts, and subjects. What this means, as Stuart Hall (1997) reminds us, is that "[w]e are all, to some degree, caught up in its circulation – oppressors and oppressed" (p. 50). My work thus sought to trace the racial subjectivities that are engendered, reproduced, and taken up by racial Others in the City of Toronto and to analyse them as historically constituted, perhaps shifting but always intelligible in relation to upholding power/knowledge and the "truths" of diversity discourse.

Lowe (2015) also writes that a "critical" genealogy "is an attempt to give an account of the existence of alternatives and possibilities that lay within, but were later foreclosed by, the determinations of the narratives, orders, and paradigms to which they gave rise" (p. 175). Lowe employs a critical genealogy to illuminate the erasure of "alternative accounts"[8] as a function of the European colonial imperative and the trajectory of liberal modernity. Importantly, she resists presenting her reading of colonial state archives and liberalism archives alongside works from C.L.R. James, W.E.B. Du Bois, Franz Fanon, Cedric Robinson, and other thinkers in the Black radical tradition as any kind of "real," more holistic account of history. Instead, it is meant to unsettle the very idea of an organized, linear world history and expose it and the knowledge(s) that arise from it as a thoroughly European, colonial construction.

The project I pursued is slightly different. I take a step back from Lowe's work, or perhaps pursue its precursor: instead seeking to trace *what actual racial norms and practices* make the domination of diversity discourse in the City of Toronto possible. Illuminating "alternate accounts," although a feature of my research, is not its focus. However, common to both of our works – at least in method – is the tracing of how Western (neo)liberal narratives emerge and "stick" via the continual management of racial difference.

I also do not seek to narrate a seamless "counter-history" of diversity in the City of Toronto, including how subjectivities are produced. Although power might radiate everywhere and continually recover itself by producing racial subjectivities, illuminating alternate accounts, paying attention to contradictions, nuances, deliberations, moments that lay outside "grand narratives," must be a fundamental part of our work, especially if we seek and claim to move beyond colonial assertions of "knowing" the Other. In tracing the racial norms and practices of diversity discourse, it was extremely difficult to avoid encapsulating everything I had seen, heard, *felt*, under one theoretical umbrella. My hope is that I give the discontinuities and contradictions that came up time and space to breathe and exist beyond the bounds of interpretation and critique.

Working with Stories

In the first phase of this study, I conducted 16 semi-structured interviews with City of Toronto staff who self-identified as racialized, part of an ethno-racial group, a "visible minority" and/or a person of colour, and who were employed at the City for at least one year at the time of the study. Recruitment of the 16 interviewees took approximately 8 months, and all interviews took place between February and October 2013. I used a snowball sampling technique (Bryman, 2001) to initiate contact with people who were known and/or recommended to me on the basis of their ability to provide their insights on diversity in the City of Toronto, as outlined in a recruitment letter. Contact was initiated with participants in departments across the City, working in political and bureaucratic offices. The sample had no restrictions on age, gender, or position.

Interviews were organized around an interview guide consisting of identifying closed-ended questions and a few open-ended questions. Through these interviews I aimed to elicit information about how racialized City of Toronto staff use and make sense of diversity in their work. Using open-ended questions enabled deeper conversations about diversity work in the City, as well as opportunities to probe further into moments of discomfort and/or tension.

One staff person dropped out approximately three days after our interview took place. As I had made clear in my recruitment letter and verbally at the outset of each interview, staff could drop out of the research at any time, with no questions asked. This interviewee emailed me to say they would prefer not to have their interview be part of my research and thanked me for our conversation. I did not probe further.

The final 15 interviews included in my study took place at various locations in Toronto – staff offices, nearby boardrooms, coffee shops, and libraries. Notably, there was hesitation from many of the interviewees to participate in a study that asked them to talk about what they feel the term "diversity" does, in and for the City. Several staff expressed fears about confidentiality and possible reprisals for their participation. Many stressed prior to our interviews that they had agreed to participate on the condition that no identifying information about them would be revealed.

Although the interviews were slated to be approximately one and a half hours, most lasted two hours or more. The conversations I had continue to resonate. Some interviewees shared their own painful experiences of racism in the City of Toronto, without probing. Some spoke in hushed tones, others held back tears. As I reflected on my notes from these interviews, what came to mind was Ahmed's (2012) assertion that those who talk about racism in "diverse" institutions often become seen as the problem, in and of the institution. These moments with staff signalled an awareness of the silencing around discussing issues of racism in the City and that speaking about racist experiences in the City is deemed "unprofessional" and/or problematic.

Noting the precarious, emotional, and sometimes contentious nature of their work, as well as how few racialized City staff there were by department, I committed to each staff person that I would not disclose any identifying information about them, including age, race, ethnic background, department, position, and number of years at the City. As such, I can offer no specific information here, other than to say that of the final 15 interviewees included in my study, 12 identified as women, and 3 as men. The number of years working at the City ranged from 1 year to more than 25. I also gave each interviewee an opportunity to choose a pseudonym in order to retain anonymity. If one was not chosen, a pseudonym was randomly assigned. All participants agreed to be tape-recorded on the condition that only I had access to the tapes, and that only I would transcribe their interviews. As promised in the recruitment letter, each participant received the raw transcripts of the interview via email, approximately 8 months after all interviews were completed.

Data collected through interviews were transcribed and analysed through coding techniques. I first conducted a line-by-line analysis of the transcribed interview materials and any ideas, insights, or questions on what was going on in the transcripts or possible links to more general issues were recorded in what Emerson et al. (1995) refer to as "memos." Miles and Huberman (1994) say that memos help to explore possible relationships and to move towards a better understanding of categories, events, and processes. Indeed, memo-ing helped me to then generate and document "themes" that emerged across transcripts.

Although my aim was to uncover how diversity discourse in the City of Toronto produces and is reproduced by racial subjectivities, I still struggle with having turned the narratives of racialized City staff into "diversity discourse data." I took their sometimes deeply painful experiences and feelings and made them part of a project that seeks to expose racialized staff's ideas of themselves in the City as being historically, politically, and racially constituted. This still feels … violent. I am also thinking here of Denise Ferreira da Silva (2015), who echoes Sylvia Wynter's critique of Foucault's theorization that "the idea of race" (p. 91) and thus domination and discourse are productive *effects* of the development of Man/the human (akin to knowing-as-being), rather than being formative of his universal existence/codification. Foucault's "missing"[9] race/coloniality as an ontological and epistemological precursor prompts Ferreira da Silva (2015) to ask "whether or not justice can be imagined from within the available modalities of knowledge, which includes Foucault's archaeological and genealogical tools along with the already known historical and scientific tools, with all the necessary erasures and engulfments they presuppose and entail" (p. 103).

Perhaps no research method completely evades the erasure(s) Wynter and Ferreira da Silva speak of. However, one risk of drawing on the tenets of genealogy to capture the materiality of race, as it is expressed in stories, is that it can further encode the "extrahuman" (Wynter, 2003, as cited in Ferreira da Silva, 2015, p. 93) – extraneous to who the modern Man is and/or what he knows – in and as text, to again underpin the qualification of the (white/European) human, all-knowing subject. In this vein, it can seem dangerous to hope that this same knowledge can be used "to speak truth to power" (p. 104).

Still, I remain committed to the idea that illuminating what the various subject positionings racialized City staff take up "do" for diversity discourse and in the interests of power is key to understanding the continuity of race in a City which, through diversity discourse, claims its undoing. Eve Tuck's (2009) letter on suspending "damage-centred" research provides a bit more clarity on my position. The letter advocates that we move away from research that necessarily portrays oppressed peoples as perpetually in pain, in order to initiate social and political change and accountability from above. Presenting Others as "broken" re-invests in them being "sites of disinvestment and dispossession ... saturated in the fantasies of outsiders" (p. 412), but also risks Others internalizing a sense of self as damaged. Of course, another risk, as Razack (2007) so eloquently puts it, is "stealing the pain of Others"; in the case of research, pain can be elicited and consumed to reproduce particular epistemological and/or ontological ends, to reproduce researcher innocence and/or criticality, or simply to elicit pleasure.[10]

Tuck argues that we should instead seek to articulate complexity and desire in our research, to disrupt categorizations of oppressed people as wholly "damaged" but also to challenge hegemonic binaries and over-simplifications which present people as either reproducing or resisting social inequities. The goal here is to pay attention to the contradictions, to "necessarily complicate(s) our understanding of human agency, complicity, and resistance" (p. 420).

I noted earlier that paying attention to complexities and contradictions is a key aim of my research. I extend Tuck's analysis here to offer that taking Others up in our research as complex, desiring subjects also allows for critical insights into the ever-evolving, productive workings of *white supremacy* – more specifically, its productive and seductive power, how it thrives in the present through the bodies of racial Others and their inclusion in social and political apparatuses that prop it up.[11] This certainly does not mean that the potential for violence in research involving Others as "research subjects" is or can ever be completely done away with. However, understanding subjectivities in terms of complexities and desires and in relation to white supremacy is crucial, especially if what we seek is any kind of social and political change centred around undoing the effects of race.

Working with Texts

The second phase of my research was guided by Foucault's (1984) insistence on revisiting "a field of entangled and confused parchments, on documents that have been scratched over, and recopied many times" (p. 76) to trace the historical and constituting effects of discourse. It is important to note here that I will refer to the City of Toronto documents I reviewed – Council, Committee, and Community Council agendas, policies, bylaws, reports, meeting minutes and attachments – as "texts," following Smith's (1999) understanding of how texts circulate in the everyday to coordinate our work, actions and lives in institutions. Smith argues that the circulation of texts reinforces particular historical, social and political practices which normalize ways of thinking and knowing, including how we come to know ourselves. We can also think about texts as a mode of production of discourse, intended to accumulate, authorize, communicate and recirculate certain meanings (Hall, 1997) or, I would argue, certain "truths."

The second phase involved following diversity discourse around in City of Toronto texts. This proved to be a huge undertaking – combing through hundreds of City of Toronto texts to trace how, when and under what terms diversity discourse moved, shifted and encapsulated, to reproduce race in the City. My "textual entry point" was the year 1995. I wanted to explore how the de-institutionalization and de-funding of many anti-racist/equity programs at the provincial level by then newly elected Premier Mike Harris influenced the City's taking up of diversity, as many authors (included the ones noted earlier) have suggested. The assumption here was that this time period would offer "a vast accumulation of source material" (Foucault, 1984, p. 76–7), as well as opportunities to observe and trace the "connections, encounters, supports, blockages, plays of forces, strategies and so on" (Foucault, 1991, p. 76) that made up diversity discourse in the City of Toronto context. I then began to move outwards, seeking to trace the pre-context(s), the specific historical conditions, the continuities, mutations and reversals of the discursive logics that would inevitably continue to bind diversity to the City, despite whatever changes to its social, political, economic and/or racial landscape.

THE TEXTS I REVIEWED

From 1 January 2006 to 31 December 2017 texts were retrieved by term (2006–10, 2010–14) and then 2014–17, using the basic search function of the City of Toronto "Toronto City Council and Committees Meetings, Agendas and Minutes" site, also called the "Toronto Meeting

Management and Information System" or TMMIS (City of Toronto, n.d.-b). An advanced keyword search was conducted, using various combinations of the terms "diversity," "racism," and "race." From the years 1998 to 2006, City texts were retrieved electronically, using the City of Toronto's (1998–2008) "legacy search" website. City of Toronto agendas, policies, bylaws, reports, meeting minutes and attachments were searched by year, using the same keywords.

Prior to 1998, City texts were available only in bound books, by year, in the City of Toronto Archives. For the years 1990–8, I conducted an archival search of relevant former City of Toronto texts using three inter-related methods: first, an index search for the terms "diversity," "racism," and "race," which I then expanded (upon recommendation by City of Toronto archives staff and/or because of the links I was seeing in my preliminary searches) to "race relations," "anti-racism," "multicultural/ism,"[12] "diversity management," "ethnic," "ethno-racial," "ethnic group," "visible minority," "racialized," "immigrant," "people of colour," "equity," "inclusion," "human rights," "Employment Equity Act," "Employee and Labour Relations," and "Aboriginal." The second method involved going through the table of contents of each Council and Committee text, looking for diversity, racism, race or terms I thought might be related, in the titles of the contents listed. Lastly, I read for references to other and/or past reports, typically listed under the "background information" section of each text. I compiled a list of these reports and included them in my overall search.

From 1970 to 1990, City texts were no longer indexed, and the ability to conduct searches by words and/or phrases was no longer available. This was the most difficult time period to navigate – because there was no indexing mechanism, I manually went through Council and Committee texts for each year, page by page. I began by reviewing the table of contents for each Council and Committee meeting, again searching for diversity, racism, race or words and phrases I thought might be relevant in the titles of each report, in addition to the terms I searched previously. These 86 additional words and phrases I thought relevant included "boat people," "human rights," "crime," "disabled persons," "equal opportunity," "Indo-Chinese Refugees," "refugee," "minority police relations," "Chinatown," "language rights," "Pakistan," "police," "police department matters," "citizen appointments," "women in male jobs," and "Ontario Human Rights Commission." About a quarter of the way through my search, I began to see that most City texts which named diversity, racism, race and/or relevant terms referenced the "Mayor's Committee on Community and Race Relations," a citizen committee of 12 struck by Mayor Art Eggleton in

1980 to address and/or make recommendations on issues of racism in the former City of Toronto. This committee appeared to be primarily responsible for addressing and/or making recommendations on issues of race, racism and/or diversity in the City of Toronto.[13] As such, I chose to focus on and trace its actions and/or recommendations.

Through my close examination, I was able to trace the beginnings of linking diversity with racism and/or race in the former City of Toronto to this Committee.[14] In Mayor Eggleton's request to establish the Committee, he writes "it is my hope that the Committee on Community and Race Relations will strive to increase the ability of *diverse* groups to communicate and interact effectively in eradicating racism and prejudice from within our midst" (City of Toronto, 1981a, p. 1054; my emphasis). One of the earlier reports of the Mayor's Committee also makes reference to an "Equal Opportunity 1979 Annual Review," a review and report of the City's efforts to achieve "equitable representation and fuller utilization of women at all levels and in all categories of the organization, as well as a full recognition of their contribution to the work of the City" (City of Toronto, 1980b, p. 8747). In this report, Alderman Sparrow amends a clause so "that the approach used to develop the Equal Opportunity program be considered for special groups such as the disabled and *minorities*" (p. 8809, my emphasis). While there were no references to diversity in the report on the status of achieving equity for women in the organization, it does appear and become linked to discussions about equal opportunity specifically for racial "minorities" in the City. These and other City texts support the position I take up in this book, that diversity discourse (re-)emerges depending on specific, local contexts, *in tandem with race*.

I also cross-referenced my search of City of Toronto texts with those of the former Municipality of Metropolitan Toronto (Metro), the upper level of a two-tier form of government which was, until amalgamation, responsible for matters of area-wide importance and "policies that would benefit both the suburbs and the central city" (Frisken, 1991, p. 272). My foray into Metro texts began with a keyword search of the minutes, reports, agendas, and by-laws for Metro Council from 1953–97, again in bound volumes, separated by year. These texts were indexed, so I followed the same three-pronged approach I had for City of Toronto texts from 1990–8. In my search, I discovered the terms "ethnic groups" and "South Asian" (1976 index), and "Walter Pitman" and "racism" (1977 index), which inevitably lead me to texts relating to the "Special Committee to consider the report of the Task Force on Human Relations."

The second method involved a keyword search of the electronic database "Reference Copies of Metropolitan Toronto Committee minutes" (City of Toronto, 1953–94).[15] Contained there were Metro Council's numerous reporting committees, including Executive, Social Services, Housing and Welfare, Planning and Parks, as well as various special committees and task forces that were formed over the years to address specific issues. Search terms used were "diversity," "race," and "racism."

Both methods led to me to a 1978 report to Metro Council from a special "all Council members" committee, convened to respond to the 1977 Task Force on Human Relations report "Now Is Not Too Late," led by Walter Pitman. The Pitman report, commissioned by the Metro Council after a series of subway beatings involving individuals of South Asian heritage on 31 December 1976, resulted in 41 recommendations to Metro Council on how to address increasing racism and racial violence in Toronto. Importantly, 18 of the 41 recommendations sought to specifically address racism in the Metropolitan Toronto Police Force. These recommendations included "psychological tests to determine racial attitudes of applicants for employment with the Metro Toronto Police Force" (Municipality of Metropolitan Toronto, 1977, p. 4), and "that greater emphasis be placed on the problem of racism and racial tension in the in-service training of all police personnel." (p. 5)

While the Pitman report makes no reference to diversity, what becomes interesting are the terms under which diversity evolves and inevitably becomes institutionalized, *through it*. Note for example the following shifts that occur when the Special all Council members Committee make their own recommendations to Metro Council, based on the Pitman report:

(PITMAN REPORT): "That Metro Council adopt a policy of making appointments to boards and commissions from visible minorities until the representation of these visible minorities on the boards and commissions has some relationship to the present mix of population in Metropolitan Toronto." (Municipality of Metropolitan Toronto, 1978, p. 1252)

(SPECIAL COMMITTEE REPORT): "That the Metropolitan Council adopt a policy of making appointments to boards and commissions from the visible minorities on the basis of the expectation that in time the composition of these bodies will reflect our heterogeneous population. That this policy be based on the merit principle which ensures that all individuals, regardless of their racial or ethnic background, should have the equal opportunity to enter into and be represented in the public institutions of Metropolitan Toronto (p. 1254)

(PITMAN REPORT): That Metro Council request a precise strategy from the
Metropolitan Toronto Police Commission for extending an intense
program of racial and cross-cultural understanding to every member of
the Metropolitan Toronto Police Force.

(SPECIAL COMMITTEE REPORT): The Metropolitan Toronto Police agree with this
recommendation and have for many years recognized the need for every
member of the Force to acquire a sound understanding of the various
ethnic groups living within Metropolitan Toronto ... these efforts will
continue. (p. 1257)

In these two examples, among many others in the Special Committee report, racism was ultimately *reframed*, setting up the terms under
which the Special Committee could recommend that Metro Council
adopt the following policy statement in response to the Pitman report:
"The Council of the Municipality of Metropolitan Toronto considers the
presence of people from a wide range of ethnic, cultural and religious
backgrounds within the Municipality to be a source of enrichment,
diversity and strength (p. 1269; my emphasis). The linking of diversity,
racism, and/or race in Metro texts began here, with this Special Committee report.

As I continued to follow diversity around in City texts, I had several illuminating moments. The first was that exploring what diversity
"does" is not simply about tracing where and when diversity shows
up in City texts. As I will describe in Chapter 3, the familiar norms
and practices of diversity discourse were recirculated in texts through
other, seemingly "more progressive" institutionalized discourses as
well. The second phase of my project thus grew into one that sought
to trace the historical racial norms and practices that, through their recirculation in City texts, regenerated diversity discourse in the present,
but could also continue beyond it.

Underpinning my approach to and analyses of diversity discourse
in City texts was Fairclough's (1993) critical discourse analysis (CDA).
Fairclough suggests that the production and interpretation of texts
shape and is shaped by the continuation of historical, discursive ideologies and practices, operating within and through broader socio-
cultural, economic and political contexts. The goal of a CDA is thus to
illuminate the discursive, ideological "traces" and "cues" in texts that
are simultaneously consumed and recirculated through texts, in and
across varying contexts. As I looked for traces and cues in City texts, I
asked, What are the broader themes that emerge through them? Have
they been contradicted, and if so, how have these contradictions been
resolved in and through texts? What do they reveal about "(i) social

identities, (ii) social relations, and (iii) values and beliefs?" (Fairclough, 1993, p. 134). How have these ideological traces, cues and City texts more broadly negotiated historical, social and/or political changes in social identities, social relations, values and beliefs and other relevant contexts, over time?

A Comparative Reading

In the final phase of the study, I read City of Toronto texts against interview transcripts, to document any similarities, differences, tensions and/or contradictions between them, and to trace how City texts might inform, be informed by and/or contravene the meaning-making processes and various positionings that racialized City of Toronto staff took up as they described their understandings of diversity in the City. This comparative reading helped me to outline and analyse the complex, institutional conditions under which power and resistance manifest and are authorized through various speech acts, texts, and identities, regulated by diversity discourse.

Butler's (2011) notion of performativity was extremely helpful here. As Butler brilliantly describes, performativity is "the reiterative power of discourse to produce the phenomena that it regulates and constrains" (p. xiii); that "it is always a reiteration of a norm or set of norms, and to the extent that it acquires an act-like status in the present, it conceals or dissimulates the conventions of which it is a repetition" (p. xxi). What struck me in my preliminary reading of City texts against interview transcripts was how the historical, racial norms and practices of diversity discourse seemed to recirculate in texts relatively unnoticed, but also determined the intelligibility, various identification(s), and subjectivities of racial Others in the City, including racialized City of Toronto staff.

This was perhaps the most revelatory aspect of the research process. Most if not all critical accounts of diversity I had read described how racial Others often fight against and/or are constrained by diversity and other institutionalized discourses, limiting if not blocking altogether many of their anti-racist efforts. I knew a kind of institutional impenetrability; a "banging-your-head-on-the-brick-wall" (Ahmed, 2012, p. 26) feeling associated with diversity work. I am not saying that this is not the case in the City of Toronto; in fact, much of the content of my interviews would, if read in isolation, support this view. However, only in this final phase did I begin to release the binaries I initially presumed I would rediscover in my research, the very ones Tuck speaks of – resistant versus complacent, powerless versus powerful, anti-racism versus diversity, even racialized versus white/ "the institution."[16] This is because I saw historical, racial norms *everywhere*; in and across City texts and in interviews, in the speech acts of those who embraced the language of diversity in their work as well as those who fought against or sought to change it.[17] It was here that I also began to think about the reproduction of the racial norms of diversity discourse as a *spatial* project, defining and binding the City as "diverse" via specific terms of racial inclusion and belonging that could at once deny and reproduce race. I thus organized my findings from the comparative reading into 6 key themes, grouping together racial norms that enabled specific subjectivities and/or inclusions: "Diversity as Morality," "Doing Diversity," "Being the Exception(al)," "Being like no Other," "Being Through Consultation," and "The Good Sell." Content from each of these themes have been integrated throughout the book.[18]

The comparative reading I carried out inevitably led to a deeper, more complex layer of understanding, where racialized City staff and other racial Others in the City are produced and included to *keep diversity going*, or more specifically, the historical racial norms and practices that make it up. Importantly, this reading complicated and also discouraged any analysis of power and discourse as wholly "top down," forced, and/or coercive.[19] Following Butler, my investigation of diversity discourse in the City of Toronto thus evolved into how it invites, enables, forecloses and assumes forms of speaking, writing, being and belonging for racial Others in the City via the reproduction of historical, racial norms. My task now is to illuminate how, when and under what terms this happens.

Organization of the Book

This chapter has offered some key insights into what is to come. The next chapter (Chapter 2) defines and expand on some of the key terms that I draw on to frame and inform the findings I present in this book. Importantly, this chapter offers a theory of belonging which also provocatively explores the roles of emotion and affect. I use this framework as a foundation from which to theorize how negotiations of belonging for racial Others in the City of Toronto and under the regulatory racial norms of diversity discourse invite specific subjectivities, emotions and desires which are structured by and grounded in the reproduction(s) of race.

Chapter 3, the first of the three findings chapters, illuminates how subjectivity and belonging for racial Others is premised on "being exceptional" in the City. This chapter traces how being exceptional is authorized through the recirculation of race via separations of the exceptional "us" (racial "insider Others") and "them" (racial "other Others," outsiders). I show how these separations are also co-authorized *spatially*, reproducing the City of Toronto as an exceptionally diverse space. Importantly, this chapter begins to map how subjectivity and belonging for racial insider Others and the reproduction of the exceptionally diverse City wholly depends on racial other Others and their claims of racism.

Chapter 4 highlights how subjectivity and belonging is also granted for racial Others "like no Other" in the diverse City who have "specialized knowledge" and/or access to racialized communities and groups. This chapter discusses some of the implications that arise when specialized knowledge of the Other gets taken up as a condition of belonging in the City, including re-authorizations of colonial thinking, interventions and practices.

In Chapter 5, I illuminate how the City of Toronto's claims to be a leader in addressing issues of diversity, racism and democracy via consultation with racial Others disguises the racial terms under which Others are invited, included and taken up. Importantly, I show how the encounter with racial Others and their claims of racism become *necessary* to the City's re-articulations of leadership on diversity and democracy. This presents an interesting paradox for the many racialized City staff who advocate for increased consultation with racialized communities.

Chapter 6 offers some reflections on diversity discourse, race, and power in the City of Toronto and tackles the question of whether or not agency is possible in the City. In this final chapter, I offer a way of thinking through agency that requires critical attention to ourselves, as subjects in and of power who are made up of collusions, contradictions, and tensions. The chapter concludes by presenting ideas for agency, strategy, resistance and *being* in relations of power, in the City of Toronto and beyond that is, as always, inspired by the hope of undoing race.

Chapter Two

Theoretical Concepts

In this chapter, I define the major theoretical concepts that you will see throughout this book. The first concepts are racialization and race, or more specifically, their relationship. A key argument of this book is that diversity discourse is not simply imposed upon "raced" bodies; rather, it recirculates normative and regulatory qualifiers that remake raced bodies and their intelligibility in the City through racialization. Defining the relationship(s) between race and racialization here provides a critical framework from which to understand this argument.

In the previous chapter I explained that while some racial Others must be included in order for the City to make itself up as "diverse," their inclusion and, by extension, belonging, is fraught with negotiations. To help explain the complexities of these negotiations and their racial and affective contents, I draw on the notion of abjection. Abjection is also vital to my analyses of diversity discourse in the City of Toronto as being dependent on the invitation to the racial Others to negotiate their belonging, ultimately, to normalize the City and the natural subject who occupies it as white.

Next are discourse, power, and space. I define each separately and then as interrelated, so it becomes possible to understand how diversity discourse in the City of Toronto has racial and spatial expressions and implications. Following this, I explain three theorizations of belonging that I draw on in this book: belonging through encounter, belonging through hailing, and belonging as a longing. Applying the first two approaches to belonging, we can begin to understand how various racial subjectivities in the City are hailed by diversity discourse into (re-)affirming particular identifications, values, and meanings, in line with familiar, historical racial norms. However, the stability of these identifications comes into question once we consider the third axis of belonging – a "longing to be someone/something else" (Probyn, 1996). Drawing on a theorization of belonging as a "longing to be" allows for a more nuanced understanding of diversity discourse and belonging in the City of Toronto, specifically how longing can produce sometimes seemingly contradictory subjectivities as well as desires and anxieties that cannot be fully contained as long as belonging in the diverse City is authorized in racial terms.

Finally, I suggest a way forward where it becomes possible to illuminate how negotiations of belonging for racial Others in the City reinvigorate diversity discourse as a racial, spatial, and colonial project. My hope is that this chapter will serve as a point of reference, perhaps to revisit when working through the various facets of my analyses, observations, and reflections you will see in the next four chapters.

Racialization and Race

A key theoretical insight that Ahmed (2002) offers into racialization, race, and the (raced) body is that race *is an effect* of racialization, not its cause. Ahmed first draws on Foucault to describe how power produces bodies:

> We can evoke here Foucault's ... notion of power as *productive*. Rather than seeing power as repressive, that is, as constraining, delimiting or prohibiting what bodies can do (which is not to say that some power does not operate in this way), Foucault argues that power produces certain effects; it is both generative and enabling.... If power is productive, then power also produces bodies. (p. 48)

Following Foucault, Ahmed argues that colonialism justified its violent quest through racializing, which produced colonized bodies as uncivilized, morally degenerate, inferior, and otherwise inherently different to the white, masculine subject. Racialization also produced the racial body as an object of knowledge, using the false marker of skin colour to secure "Black" as a racial identity with "essential characteristics" (p. 47) to be known by the white masculine subject. The grouping of humans and identities through racializing thus provided the very foundation of race, and incitements of race into discourse.

Importantly, Ahmed also posits that although race is not an intrinsic property of bodies, the "essence" of the racial body does not entirely disappear. Essence continues to be relevant and lived because race is "an effect of the very way in which we think, know and inhabit the world" (Ahmed, 2002, p. 47). The terms of the (re-)production of this "essence" in the present thus becomes a site of critical interrogation. Following Ahmed, I trace the racializing processes, incited into and by diversity discourse, that (re-)produce and rewrite the racial Other in the City of Toronto as having a certain "essence." One implication, I will argue, is that the racial "insider Other" who belongs in the City emerges, is known, and comes to self-identify in relation to the matrix of racialization, race, and essence.

I want to stress here that my intention is not to delve into the psychology of racial Others in the City. Pursuing this line of analysis would simply reproduce the colonial violence of bringing racial Others into existing fields of power/knowledge so that they become "known." Rather, by examining how subjectivities and identifications are produced within the confines of racialization and race, it becomes possible to understand the terms under which racial Others are included (and excluded) in the diverse City.

Abjection

Kristeva (1982) describes abjection as a visceral disgust and then ejection of the abject/other that threatens the identity and cohesiveness of the subject. Importantly, abjection reveals how "the subject is constituted through the force of exclusion and abjection, one which produces a constitutive outside to the subject, an abjected outside, which is, after all, 'inside' the subject as its own founding repudiation" (Butler, 2011, p. xiii). Drawing on Kristeva's theorization of abjection, Hook (2006) suggests a form of racism that is processed and realized through bodily reactions, unconditioned by discourse. The abject (which Hook is careful to state has no fixed referent, object, or essential identity) threatens the subject's psychic, symbolic, and physical integrity, which elicits repulsion, sickness, avoidance, and/or separation in the body. Abjection, as a "primal response" (p. 16), denigrates, rejects, and/or expels the abject, to separate oneself from what is perceived to threaten the stability of the subject/Self. In the context of racism, abjection manifests as a "sheer and unswayable irrationality of the fear and hatred directed at the racial other" (p. 16).

Importantly, Hook argues that the expulsion of the abject/Other is a *precondition* of the cultural symbolic, of language, and of identity. Political and discursive logics are transposed onto the bodily reactions of abjection, with and through existing social relations and interactions. Discourse attempts to contain the socially determined abject and to give it a temporary object status, but "always fails and must repeat its attempts at objectification" (Hook 2006, p. 26).

The concept of abjection allows for a more textured theorization and analysis of racial discourses, beyond texts and/or speech acts. An understanding of the visceral, urgent responses to the racial Other brings us closer to understanding, as Fanon (1952) writes, not only how and why the white man constructs the Black man, but also how the white man constructs the white man through the Black man. While abjection is certainly useful for delving into the embodied, visceral reactions to the abject/racial Other and how they are negotiated materially and discursively, its significance is, I think, heightened in the local context of the City of Toronto and under the terms of diversity discourse, where racial inclusion *is necessary*. This book explores how diversity discourse in the City of Toronto attempts (and fails) to contain the embodied reactions brought forth by local and contemporary close(r) encounters with the racial Other in the City, with a view to understanding how subjectivity in the diverse City evolves and is recuperated through the presence of the racial Other.

Discourse, Power, and Space

Discourse

What is discourse? How does it inform the way we see ourselves and how we belong? Although some might think of discourse simply in terms of the language we use, Foucault (1981) argues that discourse is "a violence which we do to things, or in any case as a practice which we impose on them; and it is in this practice that the events of discourse find the principle of their regularity" (p. 67). Thus, in addition to how discourse circulates through text and talk, we also need to pay close attention to the "physicality of its effects, in the materiality of its practices" (p. 66).

Foucault (1970) also describes discourse as an ideological force shaping knowledge of the everyday world and interests in ways that reify historical relations of power. However, to think of discourse as a repressive force, held by particular bodies over other bodies, is dangerously simplistic. For discourse and power to take hold, it must be everywhere and come from everywhere (Foucault, 1980, 1984). Importantly, subjects seldom pay attention to the repetition and recirculation of discourse in the everyday. What is required of any analysis of discourse, then, is an examination of the social, political, and historical conditions that come to (re-)produce its "truths" as natural, as a "given" (Hook, 2001).

The relationships between discourse, race, and racism have been theorized by a number of scholars. For example, van Dijk (2002) argues that racist ideologies are learned, reaffirmed, and defended through the text and talk of discourse. Those discourses are then mobilized to engage in racist practices. However, Ladson-Billings (2000) argues that discourses and their recirculation of "regimes of truth" (what is accepted as true in society) are actually constituted through race and racism. For example, "enlightenment notions of science and law did not work independent of prevailing discourses of racial superiority which allowed the dominant group to objectify the other" (p. 259).

Hall (1996) shows how colonial discourses and texts produce, solidify, and circulate knowledge about non-European, colonized peoples and cultures as "Other," and argues for an explication of how contemporary codified knowledge of the "Other" produced by the West is connected to ongoing colonial exploitation. Following Foucault, Said (1979) argues that Orientalism should be taken up as a discursive construction of the East, conceptualized through Western mechanisms of power. Said adds that the goal of Orientalist discourse is to reaffirm the superiority of the West and, more importantly, "its material continuality" (p. 216).

Of course, many others write about the relationships between discourse, race, and racism. Here, I want to focus on Weedon's (2004) discussion of humanism as a discourse. For Weedon, humanism links to other discourses of human rights and equality to convey sociopolitical spaces and citizens as tolerant and welcoming of all. However, in such contexts, subjectivities and identities fractured along racial, gendered, class, sexual, and ethnic lines navigate discourse/power/knowledge networks, which maintain historical terms of subjugation and exclusion, reinforced through hierarchical rules of recognition. Weedon argues that humanist discourses thus reproduce "different" bodies, subject positions, and identities, and also shape how subject positions and identities are taken up when navigating the need to belong in sociopolitical space.

This book complicates Weedon's theorization of the relationships between discourse, subjectivity, identity, and belonging. Specifically, I argue that belonging for racial Others in the City of Toronto cannot exist independently of the discourse/power/knowledge frameworks that structure diversity discourse, inclusion, and exclusion in space, in racial terms. I show how these racial terms simultaneously reproduce, inform, are reproduced, and are informed by the identities and subject positions that are taken up, to negotiate belonging. What I hope to make clear is how diversity discourse and negotiations of belonging for racial Others in the City of Toronto are *co-authorized*.

Power

There are lots of ways to think about power. Perhaps the most common way is to think about it is being top-down, coercive, and/or authoritarian. In this we have two "choices": conform to institutional demands and discursive moves or fight against them. Reproduction *or* resistance. However, the danger of such binary thinking, again expanding on Tuck (2009), is that we miss the complexities, desires, and complicities that underpin and reflect the *flexibility and productive power of power*, across time and space. As such, I invoke a theory of power that allows for an exploration of the relationship(s) between production and desire, and by extension, the terms under which subjectivity, belonging, diversity discourse, and the reproduction of race in the City of Toronto are re-authorized.

For Foucault (1970), discourses are conduits of power in that they entrench particular knowledges/truths about objects and subjects that also shape how people come to think about and know themselves, in line with dominant historical, social, and political interests. Foucault (1979) also coined the term "governmentality" to describe how subjects internalize, rationalize, and fulfil tasks of power. His focus here was on *conduct*, or more specifically, how governing lives and thrives through the production of subjects and the practices, activities, and behaviours they carry out. Smith (2010) expands on this, writing that institutionalizing diversity as a management principle – organizing and incorporating racialized bodies in business model terms – produces a neoliberal governmentality, where individuals learn to modify their conduct in institutions to also symbolize and prop up the tenets of meritocracy and individualism.

Some have also begun to articulate power in terms of inviting assimilation and/or complicity of racial Others. Bannerji (1997) and Thobani (2007), for example, describe how people of colour often find themselves re-deploying the hegemonic, discursive terms that are used by state institutions, mainstream organizations, and the media to obscure racism, regardless of their opposition to them, because these terms have permeated many aspects of their professional lives. At the same time, any moves to incorporate anti-racist policies and practices can be seen as a form of anger or hostility projected on whites by people of colour. This can result "in a deeper assimilation of people of colour under white supervision" (Thobani, 2007, p. 172). Puwar (2004) and Henry et al. (2017) also describe how racial Others must "play the game": exhibit the "right" language, behaviours, and social capital to gain access and thrive in institutional settings. As I have written elsewhere (Joseph et al.,

2019), what we tend to miss – especially when we are caught up in viewing ourselves as racial Others "fighting against" institutionally white spaces – is that "playing the game" is predicated on racial terms that are equally, productively racializing.

Theorizing power in these ways allows for a better understanding of how and the terms under which racial Others are included and belong, however conditionally, in "diverse" institutional spaces like the City of Toronto. These insights are also extremely important to consider when advocating, as many do, for representation of racialized and Indigenous groups in government and beyond as a way to remedy systemic racial inequalities and to make systems, spaces, and/or decision-making more "inclusive." This book builds on these theorizations of power, and in doing so, hopefully begins to destabilize re-authorizations of whiteness in "diverse" spaces.

Stoler (1995) argues that Foucault was concerned not with the changing meaning of race, "but the particular discourses of power with which it articulates and in which it is reconceived" (p. 65). She thus investigates how racial discourse appropriates different racial expressions, even emancipatory claims, and recasts them in new forms that ultimately keep truth-claims intact. A genealogy of racism(s), Stoler argues, necessitates an exploration of the reproduction of truth-claims in (and as) the continuation of historical power/knowledge configurations.

Drawing on Stoler, I offer that power is embedded in historical categorizations of race that thrive in and across discourses, time, and space in the City, but it also *collapses* a range of spatial and chronological differences and the ruptures, anxieties, and/or "breaks" that each time/space dimension might offer up. I also suggest that the ruptures that occur in interview transcripts and City texts are both a reflection and effect of power, in that although power cannot wholly contain and manage the "differences" that tug at its seams, racial truth-claims are also somehow regenerated exactly in and through moments of (its) rupture. Taken together with Ahmed's claim that power produces bodies, Foucault's notion of governmentality, and Tuck's call for an understanding of complexities and desires, my aim is to show how historical relations of power (re-)produce racial bodies to manage and contain *locally manifested* ruptures of diversity discourse in the City of Toronto.

Space

As Jacobs (1996) asserts, while theories of imperialism and (post)colonialism offer insight into their constitutive effects across time and space, attending to the space of the local is lacking. This is not to suggest that

local spaces might exist outside or beyond the technologies of imperialism and empire, making theorizing "from above" invalid to their
formations. It is that essentialist notions of space, much like essentialist
notions of identity, are constantly challenged, revised, and/or revisited
through local politics, struggles, and negotiations of place and race. It
is through attending to the local that one can see how site-specific processes incite re-articulations of the unstable racial logics of imperialism,
power, and difference that also imaginatively bound the nation and traverse the globe.

Jacobs's conceptualization of the local helps us to understand the
relationship(s) between race and space, specifically the implications of
the city as a site of "meeting" the Other, which produces imperial and
colonial anxieties in the Self (Barthes, 1981; as cited in Jacobs 1996). It
is through these racial anxieties that race and imperialism reproduce
themselves in a local context. But it is also the instability of the local context that reproduces racial anxieties. It is thus important to examine how
and under what terms local encounters with the racial Other might, even
if for one moment, exceed the binds of imperial (re-)articulation – in this
case, the City of Toronto as a "diverse" space.

It is also not enough to theorize a spatialized diversity solely in terms
of exclusion/rejection of racial claims. Certainly diversity can shape
how we think about and talk about racism in various spaces. However,
how diversity is articulated spatially can also *depend* on racism. Let me
try to illustrate what I mean here, drawing on examples from City texts
over a specific period.

In November 2002, the City of Toronto (2002b) released its three-year
marketing and branding strategy to increase its profile internationally
and at home, and to increase its global competitiveness. The strategy's
top priority was to highlight Toronto's "ethnocultural diversity as one
of its major competitive advantages and community strengths" (City
of Toronto, 2002c, p. 4), which led to the crafting of the following statement from the Toronto Economic Development Strategy, approved in
2000 by Toronto City Council:

> *Nowhere else in the world do so many people from so many different cultures,
> different ethnic backgrounds, different religions, races, creeds, colours, sexual ori-
> entations, live together in peace, harmony, and mutual respect.* (City of Toronto,
> 2002b, p. 2; my emphasis)

Developed further in consultation with five City departments and
external consultants, the City announced that its official brand would
include the theme "Toronto the Diverse," and with it, a series of

distinctive selling points: "1-of-3 GTA residents is a visible minority," "religious freedom," "inclusive," "a City of nations (Chinatown, etc.)," and "Caribana: largest West Indian event in North America" (p. 12), to name a few.

Many have written about diversity rhetoric as a kind of racial marketing ploy that depends on the commodification of "ethnic" bodies and/ or the complete erasure of racism.[1] In the case of the City's branding strategy, they would not be wrong. Just five months before the official branding strategy was released – 7 June 2002, to be exact – funding for a Toronto Muslim Youth mentoring project was approved by City Council, following crime statistics released in the spring of 2002 by the Toronto Police Service, which revealed that "hate crimes in Toronto had more than doubled after the attacks of September 11. The largest rise was in hate crimes against Muslims" (City of Toronto, 2002g, p. 2). In February of that same year, a Notice of Motion was put forward by Councillor McConnell, seconded by Councillor Shaw, concerning the vandalism of the Gayatri Mandir, a Hindu temple in Toronto. The motion's condemnation of the vandalism of the temple also served to prop up the City's diversity narrative; in a sense, yet another form of erasure:

> WHEREAS Toronto City Council has taken a leadership role to respect and to celebrate the diversity among the people of Toronto; and
>
> WHEREAS Toronto City Council has adopted many policies and programs which respect our diversity; and
>
> WHEREAS on February 8, 2002, the Gayatri Mandir at Dupont Street and Ossington Avenue in the City of Toronto was vandalized and the Murties of Lord Shiva, Shri Hanuman, Devi Lakshmi, Devi Parvati, Mother Durga and Shri Ganesh were disfigured; and
>
> WHEREAS these acts of vandalism represent a heinous crime in a place of worship;
>
> NOW THEREFORE BE IT RESOLVED THAT City Council express its distress, deepest concern and indignation about these hate crimes and join with the Federation of Hindu Temples of Canada in condemning these acts. (City of Toronto, 2002a, p. 31)[2]

These "hate crime" examples would hardly constitute the "religious freedom" espoused by the "Toronto the Diverse" brand. However, what is important to pay attention to here, in addition to these erasures, are the various attempts by the City to *elicit* claims of racism during the same period. For example, as Good (2009) reports, community

engagement forums were held in the City beginning in late 2001 specifically to discuss the backlash experienced by Toronto's Muslim community, post-9/11. Consultations in preparation for the 2003 *City of Toronto
Action Plan for the Elimination of Racism and Discrimination* were also in
full swing; "approximately 50 sessions were held across the City from
May to November 2002" (City of Toronto, 2003a, p. 3), where thousands
of residents were invited to share their experiences of racism and to give
advice on how the City could combat them. As I will discuss in more
detail later, these were all framed in City texts as more examples of how
great the City is at diversity, and as a reconfirmation of how "diverse"
the City *is*.

A delicate balance is being struck here: the space of the City is reproduced and comes to be known as "diverse" through the erasure of racism
and the explicit inclusion of those who talk about it. In this vein, my theoretical approach considers "diverse" space as a space of *containment* –
of racial bodies, experiences, subjectivities, and belonging – where
exclusions and erasures can be simultaneously denied, occluded, and
authorized, over time.

Finally, Goldberg's (1993) notion of "periphractic space" (p. 47) is
also useful to understanding the relationships between race, space,
and the making of subjects in the City. Goldberg insists that periphractic or "fenced-in" space does not necessarily have to mean mar-
ginalization in *physical* space. Periphractic space can mean limited
or no access to the social, economic, and political power of the city,
including the rights and privileges that come with authorized access.
In this case, one is located spatially at the margins of urban society.
Goldberg makes it clear: "[B]y restricting, physically or discursively,
the space of racialized bodies, certain powers and privileges remain
intact" (p. 47).

The concept of periphractic space is key to understanding how racial discourses can produce and reinforce racist exclusions, with and
through space. One question to consider in this regard: How does
diversity discourse continue to (re-)construct and manage racial Others
in periphractic space, despite their (physical and/or discursive) inclusion in the space of the City?

In the following chapters, I address this question by highlighting
how belonging in the City of Toronto is constructed in racial, discursive, and spatial terms. However, I also offer critical interventions on
the roles of emotion and affect in belonging, particularly as they relate
to the discursive production of desires to be what I term "not-raced" in
the City, and their impacts on the making of racial subjects.

Belonging

The notion of belonging has typically been theorized by scholars in relation to citizenship and identity formation, specifically how nationalist sentiments and political projects construct belonging to the nation against ethnic/racial identities that are seen to be "from elsewhere" (Antonsich, 2010; Skrbiš et al., 2007). Yuval-Davis (2007) describes how politics of belonging that bind the imaginary nation are strictly reinforced, especially during contestations of citizenship brought by those who are deemed "outsiders." As Skrbiš et al. (2007) similarly offer in their analyses post-9/11, "legitimate" forms of belonging were asserted through the further denial – symbolically, formally, and/or materially – of Muslims in the West belonging to the nation-state community.

Through Encounter

However, Ahmed (2000) theorizes belonging in relation to the *encounter* with difference. Importantly, she argues that the multicultural nation is constructed through, not against, difference: "[T]he nation still constructs itself as a 'we,' not by requiring that 'they' fit into a 'standardized pattern,' but by the very requirement that they 'be' culturally different (that they 'not be' typical)" (p. 96). Through the encounter, prior histories and regimes of difference are drawn on, to fix the stranger as either a welcomed, celebrated difference that defines a nation, or as an unassimilable, expelled threat that defines its borders and boundaries. Thus, while some bodies come to belong in the nation and others do not, they all play a role in nation-building.

Coleman (2015) draws on Ahmed's theorization of encounter to describe how the strange-other is produced as Indigenous in the Canadian context. As he argues, "[F]or many Canadian settlers, Indigenous people are *too* close to home, *too* close for comfort, *too* close to the bone" (p. 274). In this he echoes Ahmed's point: Others become "strange" through proximity, through being too close. Importantly, Coleman argues that this (fear of) proximity determines how encounters are structured, how they are interpreted and by whom, as well as what discourses we draw on to set the limits of belonging and to make each encounter (repeatedly) intelligible to ourselves.

This book questions what "truths" are (re-)produced through diversity discourse in the City of Toronto, with an understanding that diversity discourse is co-authorized with the varied subject positions brought forth in negotiations of belonging for racial Others in the City of Toronto, a space where they inherently do not belong. I read these negotiations as *necessary* to re-articulation(s) of diversity discourse and to the City of Toronto's identity as diverse, in the present. I also argue that even those who might resist/reject the language of diversity *must* be incorporated in the City that we call "diverse." From there, we must ask, Which bodies are being expelled from belonging in the diverse City, and what does this expulsion actually look like? How are these expulsions framed by the discourse of diversity? Under what conditions does the stranger become *too close* in the diverse City? Following Jacobs (1996), my approach traces local ruptures, instabilities, and anxieties as a way to expose how and when the strange(r) gets too close through encounter in the diverse City. I argue that, even as these strange(r) bodies are deemed as a threat to the diverse City, they are contained *within* its anxious borders.

However, we must also consider how proximity can be encouraged, even necessary, to belonging in "diverse" space. As Puwar (2004) warns, closer attention needs to be paid to how and why certain previously excluded bodies are now being invited, through discourses of multiculturalism, inclusion, and diversity, to come to the table. Importantly, those who are differentially located – spatially, economically, socially, and politically – can form various collectivities that are contained still within ideological apparatuses of power. Equally important to consider is that contestations and other modes of resistance can be shaped by and through state politics, policies, and discourses, permitting (limited) "entry" for a select few (Yuval-Davis, 2006). In all, Others can be brought "close(r)." But does belonging, however conditional, shape the ways in which racial Others participate in sociopolitical spaces? What kinds of identities emerge through discursive notions of belonging, and how might they engage with and be shaped through proximity?

As Hall (1996) reminds us, identity, subjectivity, and belonging are not static. Their discursive expressions are relational, contested, and intimately connected to political projects and articulations of space. I offer that in the diverse City of Toronto, the encounter produces racial expressions, identities, subjectivities, and terms of belonging that are based on and/or explicitly (re-)define Others in relation to being too close, not quite, or just close enough. At the centre, I argue, are the racial norms of diversity discourse that Others are *hailed* into negotiating.

Through Hailing

Several scholars have drawn on Althusser's notion of interpellation, or hailing, to discuss the relationships between subjectivity, identity, discourse, and belonging (see, e.g., Ahmed, 2000; Butler, 1997; Carrillo

Rowe, 2005; Lee, 2008; Weedon, 2004). To explain hailing, Althusser (1971) describes a common occurrence of an individual walking down the street and a police officer shouting, "Hey, you there!" Althusser suggests that in almost every case, the subject will turn around, acknowledging the need to respond, even if not called by name. This is the process whereby the individual becomes a subject and where subjectivity becomes linked to ideology and power. Althusser calls this "misrecognition" because there is no agreed upon arrangement, prior to being hailed. Turning around becomes an act of ideological submission.

Althusser's notion of hailing is critical to our understandings of national identity, subjectivity, and belonging in racial and discursive terms. Expanding on Althusser, Lee (2008) writes, "You are not what you say you are, you are what you are hailed. And the ways you are hailed are so familiar, so *repetitive*, that you believe that your response is of your own volition" (p. 198). Importantly, the repetition of discourse enables such hailings and responses. Carrillo Rowe (2005) additionally explains that the ways in which discourse and power hail us *and the ways in which they are hailed by us* conditions the ways in which subjects belong and are included differently in space. It is thus imperative to interrogate the inclusion of previously excluded bodies as a reflection, effect, and interplay of how subjects are hailed, and of how subjects might reproduce ideology in how they negotiate their belonging.

Through the concept of hailing, it becomes possible to see how certain racial subject positions are permitted to pass into belonging in the City through how they regenerate historical, ideological racial norms, in the present. The focus here is not upon which "kinds" of racial Others pass into belonging and which do not – again, I stress here the dangers of attempting to theorize this. This is, however, about *subjectivity*; more specifically, the terms under which subjectivity and, by extension, belonging for racial Others in the City are negotiated and authorized. I argue that these terms are historical and racial, but also that they cannot be regenerated (and occluded) without first inciting the *desire* for belonging in racial Others. What is left to be determined is how diversity discourse invites and might actually come to meet this desire, when in practice diversity discourse reproduces relations of race, and ultimately *not* belonging in the City.

Through Longing

Hook (2005) makes a critical intervention into theorizations of racism and belonging by offering up the term "technology of affect." Technology of affect refers to the ways in which we position our emotional responses to align with certain social norms, modes of inclusion/exclusion that then materialize during close(r) encounters with "difference" and negotiations of belonging in sociopolitical space. As he writes,

> We may as such assume certain affect-positions (fear, anger, irritation, love) which then become the proof of affect for a given ideological proposition, for a categorical relationship of entitlement, exclusion, belonging, etc. So: that I feel threatened by an influx of immigrants is proof enough of their moral dubiousness, proof enough also of why they – and others like them – should be prevented any rights of access. (p. 88)

Importantly, Ahmed (2004) also argues that emotions "stick" (historically constituted) subjects together through a "re-opening [of] past associations that allow some bodies to be read *as the cause of "our hate," or as "being" hateful*" (p. 120; my emphasis). In this context we can begin to theorize, as Ahmed appears to, how the encounter is deeply affective: it relies not on the embodiment of difference, but on a continuous threat of proximity. However, emotion (love, hate, fear, and so on) is also affective, in that it travels backwards, to find its causes and justifications, and sideways to where "we" are bound together through particular discourses, *against Others*. Ahmed writes,

> We can see that the affectivity of hate is what makes it difficult to pin down, to locate in a body, object, or figure. This difficulty is what makes emotions such as hate work the way that they do; *it is not the impossibility of hate as such, but the mode of its operation, whereby it surfaces in the world made up of other bodies*. In other words, it is the failure of emotions to be located in a body, object, or figures that allow emotions to (re)produce or generate the effects that they do. (p. 124; emphasis in original)

What is important here is that belonging has discursive, material, affective, and emotional components. Emotion is tied intricately to others and, as Ahmed argues, gains power through circulation and signs. Similarly, affect works through the recirculation of discourses: "[T]he more they circulate, the more affective they become, and the more they appear to contain affect" (Ahmed, 2004, p. 120).

Hook and Ahmed make important theorizations about the relationships between discourse, emotion, affect, and belonging in relation to constructing the "we" of the nation. What is required, however, is an analysis of how racial bodies/Others negotiate these discourses that, through their recirculation, might also produce and contain affective and emotional desires of racial Others *to belong*. Questions to consider in this regard: How might racial Others constitute their identities and subjectivities in negotiations of belonging in the City, and through what kinds of emotional attachments/investments? How might these attachments and investments be effected by diversity discourse? What kinds of emotions and affects might be engaged for racial Others in the encounter, and to (re-)create what kinds of subjectivities?

To help answer these questions, I draw on Probyn's (1996) analyses of the relationships between emotion, affect, and belonging as "a desire for becoming-other, a longing for someone/something else" (p. 5). "Belonging," as Probyn calls it, is a yearning that not only restricts identities from being static and/or stable, it also exposes the impossibility of ever really and truly belonging, because individuals and groups are perpetually moving between being and becoming. Subjectivity is thus an effect of longing, of being in between.

I offer that this "longing to be/come" is also an affective technology. The implication generated by this longing is that diversity discourse produces and contains the emotional and affective desires of racial Others to belong, which leads to the (co-)authorization and material-ization of multiple subjectivities in the City, in racial terms. Thobani (2007) writes, "[A]s Fanon himself experienced while living in France, the racialized marking of the body cannot be overcome, no matter the sophistication of one's deportment, the undetectability of one's accent, *the depth of one's longing to belong*" (p. 171; my emphasis). I argue in this book that diversity discourse incites the desire for "longing to be someone/something else" as a deeply affective and emotional longing to be *not-raced*.

It is important to stress at this juncture that I do not see this longing or desire to be not-raced as necessarily conscious, nor related to racial identity, or more specifically, a rejection of it. Instead, I theorize the desire to be not-raced as a deeply affective response to the discursive and material *containment* of belonging in the space of the diverse City – inviting and producing subjectivity for racial Others via an explicit dis-tancing from historical, racial norms that simultaneously define and reject racial "outsiders." Further inviting and sustaining this longing, I argue, is the encounter, wherein belonging in the City as a racial Other can be or is continually questioned, tested, scrutinized, and/or invali-dated under what Fanon (1967) calls the "crushing objecthood" (p. 82) of the continual white gaze, leading to discursive, material, and/or psy-chic renegotiations of space and place. And yet, as Fanon also reminds us, subjectivity is always-already set to prop up the liberal white world, and in this, simultaneously structures and rejects subjectivization(s) of the Other. My concern is thus with how diversity discourse draws the racial Other in to negotiate and to imagine new forms of subjectivity and be-longing, with the understanding that the various subjectivities that are caught up in yearning are regulated by diversity discourse, the space of the diverse City and the white gaze, *to refuse the "outside(r)."*

Weedon (2004) posits that a particular discourse is employed in socio-political space in order to encourage specific subjectivities, identifications, values, and attachments, to "give individuals a singular sense of who they are and where they belong" (p. 19). This, she argues, is one of the ideological functions of identity: to inhibit multiplicity and relationality of subjectivities. This book advances the idea that diversity discourse organizes and reproduces race through hailing racial Others to constitute themselves as not-raced, while simultaneously reinforcing racial divisions through their material presence and engagement. I also offer that it is through being present in space(s) where racial Others do not belong that the racial Other simultaneously effects race and feels (perhaps temporarily) transported across racial lines. My goal is to trace how and under what terms diversity discourse makes this happen.

On Diversity Discourse, Race, Belonging, and Space

The framework I have developed here undergirds my analyses of how diversity can simultaneously threaten, transform, and reimagine the City of Toronto, through the bodies of racial Others. I draw on this framework further, not only to critically examine how the City of Toronto might reify racial and discursive expressions of nation, state, citizenship, identity, belonging, and difference, but also to investigate how the City might insinuate itself in the renegotiating and remaking of these expressions.

The tendency for governments, organizations, and the media to emphasize diversity over anti-racism suggests the need to organize social, political, and/or economic spaces in ways that regenerate historical forms of privilege and status that come with dominant subject positions, and the discrimination that comes with Others. The task is thus to understand diversity discourse not only as a spatial and racial project, but also as one that reinvigorates the normative authority of whiteness and the boundaries of belonging. In the following chapters I seek to illuminate how and under what conditions diversity discourse, as a conduit of power, continues to reproduce certain bodies as "different" in the City in order to justify the continuation of historical racial norms. Building on Ahmed's understanding of how power produces bodies, I explore how diversity discourse in the City of Toronto becomes the terrain through which the "fixity" of racial Others in the City is reproduced, to keep race and power intact. Importantly, I also examine how power produces and organizes bodies in the City along racial lines at the same time that it can incite (and also contain) agency and resistance, by binding diversity discourse with emotion, affect, and the desires to be not-raced and to belong in the City. Throughout I grapple with the idea that diversity discourse gains more power, authority, and saliency *through racial inclusion*.

Chapter Three

Being Exceptional:
Moving Diversity Beyond Race

Okolie (2005) reminds us that there are advantages of racial Others interviewing racial Others, including a shared understanding of body language, emotions, anger and pain of racism that would not necessarily be shared or interpreted in the same way by a "stranger-researcher" (p. 263). In many cases, I found this to be true. However, as a former political staffer and racial "insider Other" in the City of Toronto, I was also acutely aware of how shared experiences might be unintentionally drawn out and emphasized. Kevin alluded to this in our interview. When asked why he automatically equated diversity with race in our conversation, he suggested that he "would consider the interviewer" and because "we share a common bond of being people of colour," the link would naturally occur. However, upon further probing, Kevin acknowledged that in his policy work and when he speaks about diversity with his colleagues, he often does mean race, but because he uses diversity "differently," in a more "strategic" and "innovative" way, diversity has "so much room for interpretation." While my conversation with Kevin on the conflation of diversity and race does not entirely eliminate the concern of mutual identification, it does offer a context of how any aspects of shared identity might fall outside the scope of diversity work that staff do in the City.

Something else about my conversation with Kevin struck me. In our interview, Kevin immediately used diversity and race interchangeably, but then seemed to want to obscure this when describing his own work in the City. In fact, all staff I interviewed did this. As I will show, some emphasized that connections between diversity and race are made by others – bureaucratic and political staff, agencies, organizations, residents of Toronto – but not by them personally. Others insisted that diversity in the City was about not seeing race; or, as Tania described it, "just seeing people as people." What inevitably became clear was that my conversations with racialized City staff were not just about how staff "do" diversity in the City of Toronto. In fact, our conversations revealed more about how diversity shapes and is shaped by staff's sense of *who they are*. And in this case, staff were each exceptionally capable of moving diversity beyond race.

This chapter begins the work of illuminating the production of racial subjectivities in the City of Toronto. Drawing on interviews with racialized City staff as well as City texts, I trace how the racial norms of diversity discourse enable the intelligibility of racial insider Others as exceptional, as a condition of their belonging in the diverse City. I also show how the bolstering tactics that racialized City staff engage in as they negotiate and maintain their subjectivity as exceptional in the City are premised on refusing racialization and race. And yet, because these tactics are legitimized against hegemonic conceptualizations of the racial Other, racialized City staff also inevitably re-inscribe racialization and race. I argue that these racial re-inscriptions are concealed by discursively inviting and producing racial insider Others to be not-raced subjects who belong in the diverse City.

Although the premise of this book is to trace the terms under which diversity discourse welcomes and excludes racial Others in the City of Toronto as well as how racialized City staff might take these terms up, I want to stress here that these terms are by no means fixed or seamless. I am also far too much of an optimist to align myself fully with Rose's (1996) somewhat fatalistic view that spaces of war, where contestations of regimes of subjectivity occur, offer new but inevitably containable subjectivities in the present. As such, in this chapter I also begin to delicately unpack the collusions, complexities, and contradictions that arise when one is being exceptional as powerful moments that illuminate the anxieties of diversity discourse in the City of Toronto and thus, of race itself.

Embodying Progress: Equity, Inclusion, and Intersectionality

Throughout our interviews, racialized City staff expressed strong commitments to promoting "equity," "inclusion," and/or "intersectionality" in the City and how they saw diversity as a problematic term without an incorporation of these principles. Many spoke at length about how their interpretation of diversity includes an analysis of the intersections of race, gender, sexual orientation, ability, age, geographic location, class/income, Aboriginal status, and/or immigrant status. Armed with this more critical view of diversity, racialized City staff defined their own diversity work much like Nicole did: "strategic" and "much more systemic, structural ... to change the organization."

As racialized City staff described their investments in equity, inclusion, and intersectionality, many were tenacious about using these terms to position themselves and their work as the exception to how diversity is typically interpreted and/or done, specifically how diversity means race or people of colour *for them, not me*. For example, although Flora felt that others in the City as well as the general public use diversity to "describe multiculturalism, you know, Toronto in a multicultural context," she explained how she has "had breakthrough moments" in teaching her colleagues in the City about intersectionality and how diversity is "not measured just by race." Lisa also described how important it is to her that "diversity encompasses inclusivity and intersectionality ... how various identities intersect to create unique experiences within and among individuals and groups." Because she is both a woman of colour and an activist, the first thing that comes to her mind when she hears the term "diversity" in the City is actually "women, and intersectionality of women; but for the general public, it's likely that they think of racialized people, generally ... and like, people of different cultures." As such, Lisa tries to use the term "diversity" strategically and "for political reasons" but "to also hint at intersectionality ... but then I've also come from the background of, of understanding what intersectionality is."

Others were less hopeful about their work. As Patricia offered in her critique of diversity in the City, "I find that they use the term 'diversity' as a sort of catch-all phrase when they actually mean race." In Patricia's view, the pride that is evoked through the City's motto "Diversity Our Strength" makes it difficult for her to link diversity with "equity as anti-racist, anti-sexist, anti-homophobic practices." When I asked her to describe what would happen if she did make those links explicit in City policies, Patricia responded, "I, we, we'd probably get blown out of the window."

It is worth noting here that many have critiqued the idea that institutions take up diversity, equity, inclusion, and/or intersectionality to foster institutional change. Matus and Infante (2011), for example, argue that discourses like diversity gain currency in higher education by being circulated with other attractive terms, such as "equality, equity, integration, and inclusion" (p. 294) to intensify and recirculate commitments to equality and democracy, in turn further marginalizing oppositional politics and non-normative identities. Bilge (2013) and Poisson (2018) point to how intersectionality – a term coined by Kimberlé Crenshaw in 1989 to describe the specific systemic oppression Black women face

at the intersection of multiple identities – has been co-opted and depoliticized by white liberals to signify an understanding of "different"
experiences while leaving institutional power relations intact. And as
Henry et al. (2017) poignantly argue in the context of Canadian universities, the silence around the under-representation of racialized faculty
in leadership positions, the extremely limited efforts to collect equity
data, and the lack of effort to retain racialized and Indigenous scholars
shows how diversity and equity policies are "at best ineffective and at
worst perpetuate structural racism" (p. 3).

But my concern was not with what equity, inclusion, and intersectionality may or may not do in terms of achieving "progressive"
change in the City of Toronto. What struck me was that in our conversations, staff persisted in drawing on equity, inclusion, and intersectionality to position themselves as exceptional for moving diversity
beyond race, even as they also alluded to reproducing diversity as
race in practice. Daphne described how she finds diversity particularly problematic because for everyone in the City and beyond, "white
people right here in this organization, in the media, in, you know, in
everyday life" it really means "racialized communities; for them it's
been synonymous." When she reconnects with people from her home
town, Daphne also explained how she sometimes feels as if she is in a
bit of a "time warp" and becomes frustrated because they too still see
diversity as being synonymous with people of colour. She shared how
doing international social justice work, being involved in social movements, and her work at the City encouraged her to shift the meaning
of diversity in the City to "being about achieving systemic equity,"
"to mean people who lack opportunity, access, power, on a range of
domains.... [I]t means race, yes, and it means income, it means geographic location, it means age." Yet when I asked Daphne how she uses
diversity in her work, Daphne described how she has also "used it in
the ways that most people use it, meaning racialized people ... and, so,
I think it's confusing!"

For Stacey, diversity means access, equity, and representation of "the
composition of the community you serve" and that "it's not about
race." However, when I asked Stacey if she uses the term "diversity"
in her work, she replied, "I use it in every single management meeting that I have, in terms of being mindful of things that we do. We're a
diverse group. There are cultural differences that we need to be aware
of ... and be respectful of." Stacey later explained that even though she
pushes for access, equity, and human rights language, when she is having conversations about achieving equity, she knows "it's about white
females ... it's nobody else."

In Edward's view, when the City uses words like "diversity" and "inclusion," it "only reinforces that difference and deviation from who we're colonized by, the British, white male" as the norm in the City. Yet later in our interview, Edward offered that "inclusion and inclusivity" could push the City beyond its typical diversity practices – "ads with the Hispanic guy, the Asian female" – into "putting everyone on an equal playing field ... with the same level of opportunity." When I asked Edward to explain how he thought this could be accomplished through inclusion, the same term he critiqued just moments earlier for reproducing whiteness as the norm in the City, he laughed and responded, "It's not inclusivity, it's kinda more so, like control. I don't know. It's, it's ... you put me on the spot here, Shana."

Moments of confusion like these led staff to reiterate and assert that they still saw and did diversity differently from most, and that equity, inclusion, and/or intersectionality were the means through which to, as Daphne said, "challenge the party line ... to advance something different." What began to unfold in interviews with racialized City staff led me to want to explore the kinds of subjectivities that were accessed when staff took up equity, inclusion, and intersectionality to do diversity "differently" in the City. My interest in subjectivity grew the more I witnessed staff investments in these terms continue to override any contradictions and collusions that arose in our conversations. Staff needed to maintain themselves as exceptional in the City. They needed to set themselves apart. The question that I was left with was whom they set themselves apart from, and why.

As I was thinking this through, an assertion by both Ahmed (2004) and Hook (2011) came to mind, that discourses align affective, bodily responses and emotion with historical norms to "make sense" of the encounter with racial Others. Here, I want us to consider what kinds of effects (and affects) might be generated specifically for racialized City staff as they negotiate their belonging in the City, under the historical norms of diversity discourse, which would also need to make sense of staff as racial insider Others. In this vein, we might consider how staff investments in equity, inclusion, and intersectionality to position themselves as exceptional illuminate the larger institutionalized processes that define and authorize racial subjectivity and belonging in the City, through the historical, racial norms of diversity discourse. And in this case, what I want to suggest is that staff are invited, produced, and bound through these norms to position and make sense of themselves as exceptional racial insider Others *for being the racial exception.*

Nicole and Salma further embodied the idea of being the racial exception in the City. Both were critical of past iterations of diversity, human rights, equity, and access in the City and, by extension, how they were "done" by others before them. As Nicole explained, "this time" diversity, human rights, equity, and access would be coupled with her analysis – "an analysis that I don't think many people here do" – to finally put a "strong anti-discrimination infrastructure" in place:

> And that's why I'm not mentioning diversity by itself, I'm calling it access, equity, diversity and human rights. To me, diversity without equity, access, and human rights is meaningless. Then it becomes just window shopping. So that's why I insist on calling it, it's a mouthful, I say E ... AEDHR, but you've got to call it AEDHR because it is important. Because to me the access, equity, and human rights pieces are far more important than the diversity pieces.

Although the actual work of inserting her analysis was frustrating and exhausting, Nicole felt energized by the small shifts that she was able to initiate. As she explained, "In a sense, *I'm giving meaning to diversity in a way that I don't think it has been before*" (my emphasis).

In Salma's view, past diversity work in the City was problematic because it was "just about achieving representation." Although Salma believes that hiring people from racialized communities who bring a variety of perspectives would mean "diversity is a strength in the City," she also felt that hiring and promoting particularly those with an analysis of equity, inclusion, and intersectionality was crucial to making the City "as strong as we could be":

> [T]here needs to be people in senior levels as well, that are from racialized communities, because they offer perspective and experience, hopefully. Not all of them do. *Just because they are from racialized groups doesn't necessarily mean they're going to think progressively either, right?* (my emphasis)

In our conversations Nicole and Salma set themselves apart and justified their belonging in the City by articulating a capacity for "progressive" analyses that would make the City stronger, better – a capacity that was ultimately lacking in other racial Others. These moments with Nicole, Salma, and others I interviewed show that, in taking up terms like "equity," "inclusion," and "intersectionality" to move diversity beyond race, racialized City staff also become intelligible and articulate as exceptional racial subjects who belong in the City *because they have moved beyond the limits of their own race*. To be an exceptional racial subject in the City is thus to simultaneously transgress and confirm the limits of one's race.

In being exceptional, what also recedes further from view is that staff are *produced* to make sense of themselves in this way, under the racial norms of diversity discourse and in the contained space of the City, both of which have historically normalized and reconstituted the racial Other as *the outsider*. Indeed, we can think about how exceptional staff doing diversity "differently" is inextricably tied to racial thinking, which requires that they justify their positions in an otherwise rightfully white space. The justification for their positions in the City is enhanced by their specialized knowledge and recirculation of the most up-to-date "progressive" institutionalized terms when dealing with matters of race. The troubling paradox here is that staff's desires to be exceptional change agents in the City are produced and contained by what Puwar (2004) calls "legitimate language" (p. 112), accessed and authorized almost exclusively by those in "civilized" professional white spaces. In taking up diversity, equity, inclusion, and/or intersectionality, staff thus exhibit their familiarity in and endorsement by other institutional spaces of whiteness. They are included, in essence, because they are credible racial Others.

Their production and inclusion has limits, however. As Hook (2007) reminds us, particular kinds of affective investments remain inextricably bound to racism so that even as racism becomes less explicit, even deniable, these affective investments continue racism's historical effects in the present. Racism is thus a discontinuous interchange between particular political, discursive rationalities and individualized sentiments, where "each sets in motion a dynamics of implication for the other, most apparently perhaps through the conductor of affect" (p. 265).[1] And, as Thobani (2007) also reminds us, the racialized markings of the body cannot be overcome, as long as the raced body comes into existence as proof of the white subject's superiority and knowledge.

What Hook and Thobani help us to see is that even as staff are produced to position themselves as and might desire to be exceptional racial insider Others, transgressive moments will occur as long the body is seen, felt, and/or experienced as race(d) and as out of place. At the end of our interview, Stacey recalled her experience of being racially profiled at an international airport and how this made her think that "no matter how much you want to define yourself and who you are, the preconceived notions people have of you as a racialized person will always be there." For Stacey, diversity in the City enables these preconceptions because "diversity is a preconception." As she explained, this is why, "no matter how welcoming of diversity the City might be, you go for a job interview and the assumption is oh, you know ... *here's another one.*"

Edward also shared his experience of feeling as if he was the "exception to the rule" as a racialized staff person at a community meeting because, in addition to his presence being somewhat surprising to several of the attendees, he felt they thought he should have looked and acted more in line with racial stereotypes. Edward described an experience with one attendee in particular: "My interactions with her [one attendee] should've been different, I should've been acting a different way." He elaborated on this experience, to explain his overall thinking on diversity:

> So when we're talking about diversity, and we are supposed to put everyone on the equal playing field, and then, we have a Councillor, or whoever, let's say someone from a minority community that has a power, like, is in a position of power ... that's not considered the norm. Still. They're always just an exception to the rule, type of thing, right? We still haven't changed the rule.

Corey described the questions that often come up when the City promotes racialized staff into higher positions: "Did that person really deserve the opportunity? I mean, *really*? Or is it just about fulfilling the 'optics' of diversity? Pfff. It's a joke." He continued:

> And now, what kind of burden does that person have on their shoulders now? Because I'm sure in the back of their head they're probably wondering, most people think they've earned their position. I mean, they've worked hard enough, they've achieved ... there's this little thing in the back of their head, they must think ... I gotta make sure I don't f— up ... so you're, you're always conscious of that stuff. You kind of have to be.

Staff's historico-racial affective experiences and encounters of the body figure in excess of the discursive logics of diversity in that, however momentarily, they threaten to collapse the distinction(s) between exceptional insider Others and racial other Others that make up the City of Toronto as a "diverse" space. And yet these threats are precisely what incite racial insider Others to take up being the exceptional racial subject and, by extension, reproduce the racial norms diversity discourse, as a negotiation of their belonging. The raced body thus betrays a seamless exchange between diversity discourse, desire, and subjectivity in the City, only in the end to keep the racial norms of diversity going.

Moving Beyond Race in Text

I was interested to explore how discourses of equity, inclusion, and/ or intersectionality are taken up in City of Toronto texts, specifically how they might constitute and be constituted by the varied "exceptional" positionings associated with moving diversity beyond race in the City. While countless City texts refer to equity, inclusion, and/or intersectionality, I wanted to focus on texts that introduce these terms as a way to shift conversations about diversity, race, and/or racism in the City, to support and/or reflect the view of many staff that the insertion of these terms is a strategic way of moving diversity beyond race. I found that while equity, inclusion, and/or intersectionality texts *did* introduce more firm language about racism – not necessarily tied to changes in recommendations and/or action – in many texts the familiar racial norms of diversity discourse seeped through and continued to circulate. I have included some examples below.

Equity

The term "equity" appears in City of Toronto texts largely to address the under-representation of racialized and other marginalized groups as employees of the City, or to address barriers to accessing City services. For example, in 1975 the City of Toronto created an Equal Opportunity Program to achieve "more equitable representation and fuller utilization of women and men at all levels and in all categories of the organization, as well as a full recognition of their contribution to the work of the City" (City of Toronto, 1980a, p. 8747). In the 1980 annual review of the program, Alderman Sparrow recommended that the program be extended to include "special groups such as the disabled and minorities" (p. 8809), which was subsequently expanded to "native people, people with disabilities, racial minorities, and women in the civic workforce," in response to the *Equality in Employment: A Royal Commission Report* by Justice Rosalie Abella (City of Toronto, 1992a, p. 69).

After a full-scale corporate review of Equal Opportunity policies and practices during the period 1986–90, the City set up a plan to expand its equal opportunity initiatives to achieve *equity* because:

(A) People with disabilities have not been hired at the same rate as other designated groups;
(B) Designated groups have been, on the most part, hired into temporary positions, but they are underrepresented in external hiring into the permanent workforce;

(C) Designated-group employees have less seniority and have histori-
     cally faced systemic barriers to employment; they do not, there-
     fore, have equitable access to internal opportunities for mobility
     and promotions within the civic workforce. (p. 69)

The Toronto Mayor's Committee on Community and Race Relations[2]
also submitted their comments for the corporate review, explicitly pointing to racism as a significant factor in the unequal hiring, retention,
and pay practices in the City. In their submission, the Committee provided strong evidence that, despite the City's efforts, "salaries among
racial minorities in the civic workforce have been declining relative
to whites," racial minorities continued to be under-represented in the
permanent employee category, and "in the permanent civic workforce,
Native people are represented by less than half their proportion in the
city labour force as a whole (2%)." In closing, the Committee argued
that "the City of Toronto still lags behind other employers in the hiring
of racial minorities and Native people" (City of Toronto, 1992a, p. 75).
     On 23 March 1992, City Council responded. To achieve equity and "in
order for the City to maintain its leadership role and its accountability
to the diverse community it serves" (p. 70), Council recommended:

1. That City Council authorize the establishment of a corporate fund for
   internship/bridging/apprenticeship positions to enable designated groups
   to gain access into occupations where they are underrepresented.
2. That City Council authorize the Executive Director of the Management Services Department to ensure that *training and development
   strategies* give designated group employees the *knowledge, skills, and
   experience to compete successfully* for management vacancies in the
   permanent workforce. (City of Toronto, 1992a, p. 70; my emphasis)

Here, any systemic barriers to employment identified by the corporate review and the Toronto Mayor's Committee on Community and
Race Relations are effectively erased by assigning designated groups
a lack of skills, knowledge, and experience. But perhaps not all designated groups. As I discovered in my review of subsequent "equity"
texts, internships, training, skills development, and mentoring programs are overwhelmingly recommended for racialized, immigrant,[3]
and Native/Aboriginal/Indigenous groups in particular, to improve
their access to and mobility within the City's workforce.
     For example, the City of Toronto's (2014a) *Aboriginal Employment
Strategy*, which "supports the City's ongoing commitment to equity
and diversity," sought to ensure "that the representation in the Toronto

Public Service workforce mirrors the representation of Aboriginal peoples in the City" (p. 3). Recommendations in the strategy to achieve representation of Aboriginal peoples included mentoring, skills training, and apprenticeships "for Aboriginal residents to meet qualifications for specific City of Toronto jobs" (p. 5).

Through this deliberate association of racialized, immigrant, and Aboriginal/Indigenous Others with a lack of skills, knowledge, experience, and training in and across City texts, racial Others are read and rewritten as having a racial "essence" that renders them naturally inferior and incapable. Of course, this narrative is not new. But the recirculation of racial lack *unless* racial Others are mentored by those who are more established and capable additionally draws on and reproduces discourses of moral obligation and paternalism that are rooted in colonial, racial thinking, and also reproduce a natural association of the somatic white, male, upper-/ middle-class norm (Puwar, 2004) in the City with power, knowledge, and capability. The denial of racism in the City through lack, embedded in the language of equity, is thus premised on historical narratives that are familiar but also *reconstituting* of the diverse City as a rightfully white space.

Significantly, the circulation of City "equity" texts that recommend mentoring also co-produce racial and/or immigrant lack with Aboriginal lack. As Coleman (2015) asserts, (fear of) proximity and settler guilt determines how encounters with Aboriginal people are interpreted and by whom, as well as what discourses we draw on to make each encounter repeatedly intelligible to ourselves. In City texts, conflating Aboriginal, racial, and immigrant Others under the racial norms of diversity discourse – continued through equity – is an attempt to "make sense" of ourselves and the City as being beyond our colonial "past" and as non-violent, through the erasure of Aboriginal bodies who put these senses most at risk. Aboriginal Others are thus (re-)produced as "diverse" to further their erasure.

Equity also appears in City texts to frame barriers to access for racialized groups in terms of language difficulties and/or "cultural" differences. For example, in May 1991 the City of Toronto created the Multicultural Access Program (MAP) in response to problems that members of ethnic and racial minorities had encountered in getting access to municipal services (City of Toronto, 1990b). During the implementation phase of MAP, Mr. Allan Rodney of the Native Canadian Centre submitted his concerns about the focus of the program:

> That the emphasis on multiculturalism may obscure the real issue of concern to Native people which is *the issue of racism*. The document is very soft

in its treatment of racism and should be more explicit in its condemnation
of racism and the City's intention to eradicate racism at both an institutional and a personal level. (City of Toronto, 1991b, p. 251; my emphasis)

In response to the assertion of Mr. Rodney and others that the program was not adequately addressing racism in the City, an external consultant was hired to evaluate MAP. The consultant recommended that
the program be renamed "the Service Equity Program (SEP)," along
with a series of initiatives that would "make City of Toronto services
available to racial and ethnic groups" (City of Toronto, 1992b, p. 120).
These initiatives were to resolve what he identified as the core reasons
why racial and ethnic groups were inhibited from accessing City services: language issues, "organizational complexity" (p. 120), and the
lack of racial/ethnic representation in the City's workforce (which City
Council later sought to resolve through mentoring). Although the consultant also requested that City policies and procedures be reviewed
for discriminatory barriers, he offered no specific direction on why,
how, or when this would be done. Again, the City was absolved from
any responsibility for racism by drawing on familiar, historical racial
norms that, through their recirculation in City texts, remain largely
unquestioned.

It is important to note that in 2006, City Council passed a resolution
that Equity Impact Statements accompany all City reports, to ensure
that City departments were identifying and working to remove barriers
to access for equity-seeking groups and that addressing these barriers
was also prioritized in City decision-making (City of Toronto, 2006). In
more recent years, the efficacy of these statements has come into question (see, e.g., City of Toronto, 2014c). However, in some cases, City
staff have used Equity Impact Statements to explicitly refer to the social,
political, and/or economic exclusion of various groups in the City.

For example, the Equity Impact Statement for the *TO Prosperity:
Toronto Poverty Reduction Strategy 2017 Report and 2018 Work Plan* (City of
Toronto, 2017c)[4] outlines how the ongoing "racialization, feminization,
and geographical concentration of poverty in Toronto" (p. 3) formed
the basis for recommending that a series of program and service initiatives be considered as part of the 2018 budget process.[5] Importantly, the
Report/Work Plan goes on to directly challenge the historical conflation
of racialized and immigrant that also underpins the City's diversity narrative: "This [higher rates of poverty and lower incomes among racialized groups] *is not simply a function of visible minority groups being newer
to the country*" (p. 4; my emphasis). Of course, Equity Impact Statements
do not guarantee that the City will take any action; in the case of the

Report/Work Plan, the majority of budget asks were not approved by Council. It is thus worth considering what the impacts of these few "intervention" texts are, especially as they are produced and emanate largely in isolation in the City. If indeed these texts exist, circulate, and are taken up by the City-at-large *as exceptional texts* – perhaps prepared by exceptional racialized staff – the question we must return to is about the relationship(s) between race, space, being exceptional, and direct action to address racism; again, what these exceptional moments and siloed spaces do for the City, for staff, and if their effects (and affects) are such that they might largely *contain* action.[6]

My search also led me to quite a few texts describing the City as a leader, role model, and/or exceptional at achieving "equity."[7] For example, in 2009 the City crafted a *Diversity and Positive Workplace Strategy* in response to a report from Ryerson University, which detailed the "underrepresentation of visible minorities in the supervisory level at the City of Toronto" (City of Toronto, 2009a, p. 4). The City's response was to implement a strategy that would build upon its current "leading edge best practices in equity": the Black African Canadian Employment Equity Pilot Project (mentoring program for Black/African Canadian employees), Career Bridge (internships for internationally trained professionals) and the Profession-to-Profession Mentoring Program (mentoring for immigrants) (p. 4).

Here, the *Diversity and Positive Workplace Strategy* draws on the language of equity to continue the City's legacy of linking the lack of racialized and immigrant employees in the City with a lack of knowledge, skills, and training. However, the Workplace Strategy also recommended that City supervisors and managers be trained on "Inclusion in the Workplace: Race" and "Duty to Accommodate" (City of Toronto, 2009a, p. 2), to "capitalize upon the Human Rights Office's trends analysis to provide training to prevent complaints" (p. 5). While this recommendation hints at racism in the organization, no details are provided on why this particular recommendation is offered, what the "trends" are, what the complaints are, or why these trainings are specific to race.

As I discovered, the City is often written about and taken up as a leader in equity through occluding institutional racism. A lack of skills, knowledge, training, language, and/or cultural adaptability continues to be identified and recirculated in City texts as reasons why access for racialized groups is limited, despite claims that racism is the core issue. But there is also something to be said for the fact that, in and across several City texts, the City's leadership in achieving equity is tied almost exclusively to the City's ability *to recognize and address lack in racial Others*. The City's stellar reputation thus depends on the reproduction and familiarity of historical racial norms as well as what racial and discursive anxieties they alleviate, across multiple contexts.

Inclusion

The word "inclusion" appears in City texts largely in terms of seeking to increase the social, political, and/or economic participation of marginalized Torontonians in the life of the City.[8] Notably, "inclusion" rarely circulates in City texts without equity, diversity, and/or human rights language. In the few times the language of inclusion does appear by itself and in reference to race/racial barriers in the City,[9] it also perpetuates and recirculates racial lack.

For example, in the *Recreation Service Plan 2013–2017*, inclusion is listed as one of four guiding principles that would help the City's Parks, Forestry, and Recreation Department to further "recognize diversity and encourage participation of marginalized and racialized people and groups" (City of Toronto, 2012a, p. 8). To gauge just how inclusive recreation programs and services were, a survey of residents was conducted that asked if the City's recreation centres were *"welcoming to newcomers, accommodating to those with a language barrier, and meeting the culturally diverse needs of Torontonians"* (p. 57; my emphasis). Here, potential barriers to access and participation in the City's programs and services are already "pre-framed" as language difficulties and cultural differences, not racism. Importantly, this pre-framing shaped the survey in ways that occlude and/or could pre-emptively discourage claims of racism in the City's recreation centres and programming.

And yet racism still pokes through. Included in the collation of survey data was the observation that "some people from racialized backgrounds were less satisfied" (City of Toronto, 2012a, p. 47). This is the only place in the 92-page Recreation Plan where racism and/or racial barriers are hinted at, yet there is no discussion beyond this; only "these results tell us that the foundation is in place, but that we cannot lose sight of active inclusion as a principle of service" (p. 47). This is what I found particularly interesting: the language of inclusion methodically divorces the City's recreation centres and programming from racism/ claims of racism right at the outset, specifically through the survey sent out to Toronto residents seeking to determine if services and programming were instead "culturally" appropriate and/or accommodating to various forms of racial lack. Yet once racism in the City's recreation centres and programming is identified by the survey, inclusion – or "active inclusion" – is invoked as the way to address racism. In short, a report determining that the City's "inclusion" paradigm might not work also then determines and confirms that inclusion works.

In addition, the brief "hint" about racism is, in the report, placed immediately adjacent to the following quote from a survey respondent (and in larger text):

> It is very challenging to get information and know what is available as a newcomer. I needed someone to introduce me. It was easier after I knew my way around. I imagine it would be even more challenging if I didn't speak English. (City of Toronto, 2012a, p. 47)

In this text, not only are claims of racism shrunk to one line, the strategic placement of it also suggests an attempt at further occlusion/erasure. Also in this text, as in others, the language of inclusion occludes barriers to access and participation for racial Others in the City through further normalizing Others as the site of language difficulties and/or cultural inadaptability. Importantly, recirculating lack in these ways – which, as I will show throughout this book, the City does repeatedly – also assumes and naturalizes a conflation of racialized and immigrant, and furthermore, with those whose first language is not English. These assumptions are deeply raced, in that they assume that all racial Others are immigrants and experience "difficulties" simply because they are *not from here*. In this, the white male somatic norm is again naturalized in the diverse City, as one who rightfully belongs and is also innocent of racism.

Intersectionality

The term "intersectionality" appears in City texts to make gender issues a priority in the City, which, as I discovered, can also be premised on racial lack. During the 2002 public consultations for the City's *Plan of Action for the Elimination of Racism and Discrimination*, the Chair of the City's Community Advisory Committee on the Status of Women, City Councillor Pam McConnell, introduced the concept of intersectionality as a way for the City to account for the different experiences women and men have in the City's programs and services. Councillor McConnell asked that a gender-based intersectional analysis tool also be developed that would examine the differential impacts of policies and services on gender identity as they intersect with other identities. Importantly, Councillor McConnell saw this tool as a way to ensure that the City did not make women's issues peripheral when discussing issues of racism (City of Toronto, 2002f).

As Councillor McConnell was pushing for an intersectional analysis in the City, she also put forward a Notice of Motion to the October 2002 meeting of Toronto City Council regarding the case of Amina Lawal and, more broadly, Sharia Law in Nigeria (City of Toronto, 2002e). The Notice of Motion asked Toronto City Council to convey the concerns of Torontonians regarding the case to the Prime Minister, and to help petition the government of Nigeria to ensure that the "horrific sentences against Amina Lawal" (p. 2) were not carried out. In her Motion, Councillor McConnell issued the following statements:

> WHEREAS the people of Toronto have been in the forefront of efforts to create a compassionate society and have demonstrated a long commitment to women's equality and human rights; and
>
> WHEREAS in March 1883, Toronto City Council supported the founding of the Toronto Women's Suffrage Association at a meeting held in Council Chambers; and
>
> WHEREAS in 1909, a member of Toronto City Council presented a petition of more than 100,000 signatures to the Premier of Ontario in support of women getting the vote; and
>
> WHEREAS in 1973, the City of Toronto established a Mayor's Task Force on the Status of Women, which brought about major changes in the delivery of municipal services, particularly health care for women and children, day care, employment equity and equal pay; and
>
> WHEREAS Amina Lawal, a 30-year-old Muslim woman was sentenced to death by stoning by a Sharia court at Bakori in northern Nigeria, for having a child outside of marriage; and
>
> WHEREAS the sentence on Amina Lawal has provoked a world-wide wave of shock and revulsion;
>
> WHEREAS the sentence imposed on Amina Lawal constitutes torture and is cruel, inhumane and degrading and runs counter to international human rights standards; and
>
> WHEREAS Toronto City Council takes a leadership role in the fight of all forms of discrimination and is committed to human dignity, social equity, social justice and solidarity.... (City of Toronto, 2002e, pp. 1–2)

Although Councillor McConnell introduced intersectionality with the aim of analysing "the needs of our diverse communities" (City of Toronto, 2002f, p. 3) as they intersect with gender, in practice, intersectionality was taken up to *prioritize* gender in the City, under specific terms. In the case of the Motion, prioritizing issues of gender was undergirded by the reproduction of colonial, racial thinking, positioning "them" – a primitive, backwards, uncivilized, sexist/misogynist/patriarchal Nigeria – against "us," the diverse City of Toronto, an exceptional space where progress for and solidarity among women are of the utmost importance.

I am reminded here of Smith's (2010) assertion that the pursuit of equity in the Canadian academy has historically been about pushing for *gender* equity, a "women first" (p. 37) approach that has almost exclusively benefitted white women. In a similar vein, intersectionality was co-opted and institutionalized in the City of Toronto in a way that made issues at the intersections of race and gender peripheral (if not completely non-existent) unless and until issues of gender could be extracted, isolated, and then serve as proof of the need for their ongoing prioritization. In this, the multiple, oppressive experiences of racialized women inevitably served to reinforce a longstanding political agenda seeking equality/equity for white women in the City.

Significantly, the splitting off of issues of gender from issues of race also enabled the reframing of the experiences of racialized women because they were outside the bounds of gender and/as whiteness. For example, the City's Parks, Forestry, and Recreation Department issued a response to the report *If Low Income Women of Colour Counted in Toronto* (Khosla, 2003), which drew on an intersectional analysis to show how women of colour in low-income neighbourhoods across the city, including immigrant and refugee women, faced barriers to accessing public recreation opportunities. The department's response assured that with women being "an identified target group within the access and equity agenda" in the department as well as the City at large, Parks and Recreation was "committed to increasing the variety and number of recreation opportunities (i.e. sports, fitness, and other activities) for women" (City of Toronto, 2004, p. 3).

The department then reiterated several of its *existing* low- to no-cost recreational opportunities for women and for recent immigrants. In this, low-income racialized women were pigeonholed as either women or immigrants, leaving little room for an understanding of the specific experiences and/or differential access for low-income racialized women who were not immigrants or who might still face barriers, despite the department's numerous "women-only programs" (p. 3). However, as a *cultural* initiative for women, the department offered those who were new Canadians, "especially those from warm climates, opportunities to learn and play Canadian winter sports" (p. 3).

Intersectionality was thus taken up within existing diversity frameworks to render all low-income women of colour as immigrants, culturally "different," and/or needing to adapt. In addition, the response's claim that women-only programs were already in place and were providing many opportunities for women to "come together, to share, to show support and to socialize" (p. 3) discounted the very premise of Khosla's report: that low-income women of colour in Toronto were overwhelmingly *not* participating. The question of *which women* were participating in women-only programs (and by extension, which were not) also became irrelevant under the historical terms of intersectionality and gender in the diverse City, which almost exclusively bypasses race by relying on its familiarity in the present, to abject and exclude racial other Others and their experiences.

So what does this all mean? As I have begun to illuminate, recirculating a lack of skills, knowledge, experience, language, and/or cultural adaptability in City texts is how the City reinscribes and normalizes the historical, racial norms of diversity discourse, in order to continue to disavow the racism that would otherwise threaten its status as an exceptional and diverse space. I give several more examples throughout the book. However, in the context of equity, inclusion, and intersectionality, I ask that we pay particular attention to how *experiences of racism in the City are the trigger for the incitement and reproduction of these racial norms*. In this, a paradox emerges. In inviting and seeking to advance critical insights into systemic barriers to access and other forms of racism in the City, equity, inclusion, and intersectionality can also risk re-authorizing and recirculating historical, racial thinking in the present and ultimately the City of Toronto as a space that is innocent of racism.

The texts I have presented are not to be taken as representative of what *all* equity, inclusion, and intersectionality texts might "do" (or not do) in the City. The key takeaway I wish to put forward – in line with my project's aim to trace how racial norms and practices continue to operate and through what means in the City – is that the familiar racial norms of diversity discourse can and *do* continue to circulate through these "more progressive" terms. An additional paradox thus arises when we consider that equity, inclusion, and intersectionality are also bound to and further legitimized by staff bolstering themselves as exceptional, to justify their belonging in the diverse City. Staff take up equity, inclusion, and intersectionality in part to *refuse* their own racialization in the City, only to *reinscribe* and justify the racialization and abjection of racial other Others on the "outside." Although there were moments of contradiction and collusion in my conversations with racialized City staff on what equity, inclusion, and intersectionality actually do in the City, I suggest that these contradictions and collusions become less evident (or relevant) because many staff understand themselves to be exceptional, agentic subjects. Taken together, City texts and interviews on equity, inclusion, and intersectionality point to important processes of refusal and re-inscription and how they are *co-authorized*.

As Davies (2000) writes, our desires for freedom, autonomy, and agency in institutions can lead to an idea of ourselves as being outside of power, which is integral to the continuity and occlusion of "both the discourses and subject positions made available within them" (p. 55). Importantly, the desires for freedom, autonomy, and agency continue to be made relevant and are validated in the space of war (Rose, 1996) where discourses and power are contested. In a similar vein, I suggest that although the desires to be exceptional and agentic racial subjects in the City might be produced through diversity discourse, they intensify and are validated through the recirculation of equity, inclusion, and intersectionality, enabling, racialized staff to position themselves further outside of diversity discourse, race, and power in the City. Perhaps the most difficult contradiction to consider here is that staff's agentic positionings outside of power, as *an effect* (or affect) *of* diversity discourse, race, and power in the City, can further conceal the failure of equity, inclusion, and intersectionality to move diversity beyond race.

At this juncture, I feel it is necessary to again stress that the purpose of my discussion on contradictions and collusions is not to blame racialized City staff. Instead, I see the contradictions and collusions that arose in conversation and in City texts as sites of illumination into the productive force of diversity discourse to simultaneously create the perception of an individual, autonomous, and agentic Self and conceal how that Self comes to be spoken into existence through race and power. Earlier in this chapter, I argued that moments of tension in my conversations with staff are powerful in that they show how the production of the exceptional racial subject in the City can never be fully complete as long as the body is seen and felt as race(d) and out of place. In other words, the subjectivization of the exceptional racial subject in the diverse City cannot fully contain the materiality of race.

The argument I have been carefully building here is that contradictions, collusions, tensions, and/or anxieties do not preclude the possibility of strategy or agency for racialized staff in the City; rather, *they are the beginnings of what makes agency possible*. As Davies (2000) argues, agency occurs when we recognize that desire is integral to the reproduction of discourses that make up our "essential Selves" (p. 64) in relations of power. Our work, then, is to expose the desires, positions, and practices that are mired in contradictions, so that our essential Selves and the discourses that contain them begin to unravel. Following Davies, I suggest that an awareness of contradictions, collusions, tensions, and anxieties also makes visible the powerful investments in and continued relevance of race in the diverse City, including the terms, discourses, and bodies through which it thrives and is occluded.

Not Seeing

In my interviews with racialized City of Toronto staff, tense and at times contradictory moments also arose as staff were describing the City of Toronto as diverse, colour-blind, and welcoming to all. Tania began our conversation by describing how she felt very lucky to live in Toronto, where everyone is so "welcoming, open, and open-minded." However, Tania also admitted that her identity and sense of belonging in Toronto is tied to how she views experiences of racism in the city, including her own:

> I have that kind of mentality, so I guess I don't even really allow myself to see anything but like, of course, I'm Toronto. Like, I'm the city of Toronto because I was brought up here. Yeah, so I don't really see it. *I don't let myself see* ... like even with the, when you were asking me about the outsiders, like, there is obvious racism and there is stuff, but I'm like, no. Like, it's OK. Like, only see the good. Is that weird? Does that make sense?

What Tania was describing was something I later understood to be quite central to my analyses of diversity in the City: identity, subjectivity, and belonging for racialized City staff are discursively and *spatially* constituted. As Ahmed (2007) explains, certain bodies are included, belong, and constitute what a space "is" and is known to be in discursive terms (i.e., "diverse"), while others who contest what it is are deemed a threat. At the same time, how a space is articulated and known in discursive terms (i.e., "diverse") shapes which bodies are included and belong in that space, and under what conditions. Following Ahmed's logic, we can begin to understand how discourse, space, belonging, and the granting of subjectivity for racial Others in the City are co-produced.

In Tania's case, not letting herself see race/racism, which she viewed as a necessary function of belonging as a "Torontonian," also shaped how she took up being racialized staff in the diverse City. Despite knowing that she was "filling the [skin colour] quota" and was "being used for, because of my background," Tania thought it was more important to continue "to find the silver lining" in her work, including that she "gets to be on the inside."

Still, tensions crept in. As Tania was describing how she felt when she was officially hired by the City, racial anxieties bubbled to the surface:

I was just, I was happy that [her supervisor] accepted me as well. *Hey, that's weird, that I would think that! That I had this whole like, oh, they accept me.* Anyhow, now that I'm here, I'm gunna show them what I can do. (My emphasis)

We can begin to get a sense here of how staff "not seeing" is integral to their being exceptional and to their belonging in the diverse City. However, what really captured my interest in my conversation with Tania and others I interviewed was how the co-production of the diverse City and the exceptional racial subject who does not see race/racism also depends on the ongoing containment of affective, embodied responses associated with being race(d) and out of place in the diverse City. In interviews, staff's affective responses to being race(d) – e.g., "Hey, that's weird, that I would think that!" – repeatedly collided with their almost utopian view of the diverse City and by extension, their positionings as exceptional racial subjects. In continuing to explore the co-production of the diverse City and exceptional "not seeing" subject below, I emphasize and then unpack some of these affective responses so that we can better understand how diversity is revitalized in the present through the bodies of racialized staff in the City.

In Michelle's view, the City's motto "Diversity Our Strength" conveys how people in Toronto come together, live together, and work together, regardless of skin colour, background, culture, or religion. Working in the City of Toronto has been a prime example:

Everyone's friendly. You know, you could see a Chinese person walking down the hall, they'll get treated the same as the white person or the Black person ... [W]e're in a professional environment where we understand that, you know, everyone deserves respect and should be treated with equity.

As our conversation on diversity progressed, however, Michelle conceded that, in terms of who works in the City, it "really is very, very white." In fact, Michelle returned to this point a few times during our interview, yet when I asked Michelle to share her thoughts on why the City is so white, she replied, "It may be that my judgment is wrong." Later, she returned to the question: "I don't know what it is, to be honest. I don't know why it's like that." For Michelle, racism in the City and/or the City's hiring practices was simply not a possibility.

Michelle also drew on her experiences helping racial Others to access City services to further justify her view that racism does not exist in the City. As she described it, "they" often say "I am being discriminated against blah blah blah" if they do not get the help they want. As such, Michelle sees claims of racism largely as "a card that people try to use" to get more attention. Equally frustrating for Michelle are racial Others who assume that she will help them or be more sympathetic to their needs "because I'm [her ethnicity] or because I'm [her skin colour]." For Michelle, diversity was about change, about moving beyond racial differences. The problem in the City was not racism; rather, it was the people who continued trying to make race and racism relevant.

Stacey was also adamant that she "never looks at people in terms of their race" but that some racialized staff do and try to use it to their advantage. For example, some staff who share the same racial background as Stacey will often "circumvent their supervisor" and "jump the queue" to gain direct access to her for help with work issues. In fact, as Stacey explained, it is quite common for "visible minority" staff in departments across the City to want direct access to their "visible minority" supervisors, but because she personally values competency and skills above all else, she maintains strict boundaries: "If you're not skilled at your job, forget it! I'm not rewarding you for bad behaviour!"

Implicit and perhaps explicit in Stacey's comments is the sense that other racialized City staff were "jumping the queue" because they were unskilled and/or bad at their jobs, not because of racial tensions and/ or racism that might exist in various departments across the City. However, the undercurrent that ran throughout my conversations with Stacey, Michelle, and others I interviewed was that racial Others become the problem in the diverse City when they see race/racism, because seeing race/racism means seeking special treatment. In the diverse City, *seeing race/racism is an attempt to jump the queue.*

Staff thus positioned themselves as exceptional racial subjects for having "made it," in the City and beyond, entirely on their own merits. They had the "right" education, skills, language, behaviour, and social capital (Henry et al., 2017; Puwar, 2004), which *earned* them a place in the City – again, a space where racial Others would otherwise not belong. In doing so, however, staff were also implicitly aligning themselves with the historical, racial narrative of diversity discourse: other racial Others were not participating and/or employed in the City because they lacked the proper education, language, culture, skills, and knowledge.

At certain moments, staff felt compelled to separate themselves even further from racial other Others who "see." They invoked examples of how bad/backwards racial other Others were for seeing race/racism, again confirming the historical racial norms that underpin the diverse City narrative, but this time also justifying the denial of racial other Others who make racial claims. In my review of interview transcripts, I was able to trace how staff reinforced this separation most in moments when, by other racial Others seeing race, staff were *seen as and/or felt race(d) too*. In "seeing," racial other Others got too close. Importantly, these were moments when, again, the distinction(s) between the exceptional insider Other and the racial other Other who make up the City of Toronto as diverse began to dissolve.

In this vein, I want to suggest that staff emphasizing their separation from "them" is an effect of the production of the exceptional racial subject in the City, which, as I argued earlier, cannot fully contain the materiality of being race(d) and out of place. In this case, staff making these distinctions clearer further contains racial other Others who, in seeing race/racism, ultimately betray the production, positioning, and desires of staff as exceptional, not-raced subjects who belong in the diverse City. Staff thus refuse their own racialization and race in the diverse City by locating them in racial other Others who "see." In doing so, staff uphold and continue the racial scripts of diversity discourse that insist on the irrelevance of race and racism in the City. Yet in these moments we also begin to understand how some staff seeing or even naming race and racism in the City is contained by the threat of them *becoming* race(d). Again, I emphasize that these affective moments are powerful in that they expose the racial anxieties of diversity discourse and the desires for an essential Self beyond the binds of race in the City that suture them, however temporarily.

What I have described thus far are some of the insidious ways in which racialized staff are produced as exceptional for not seeing race and racism in the City. I would be remiss at this point to not also discuss the more obvious, tangible ways in which some racialized City staff are "encouraged" to not see. For example, in our interview, Alison described how she is not invited to dinners or BBQs with management because management does not know if she will "play ball" and "have their backs" when managing issues of diversity: "whether when the chips are down, I'm going to align myself with them, or am I going to be the person that's going to be the whistle-blower, right?"

Puwar (2004) writes that when racialized bodies talk about racism in diverse institutions, they are engaging in "renegade acts" (p. 138). Those who call attention to racism risk whatever safety, security, and racial anonymity they have built in their careers. In diverse institutions especially, speaking about racism is not only unjustified, it is offensive.

After my years as political staff in the City, I can vouch for the claims Puwar is making. Even so, the idea that racialized staff and other racial insider Others cannot talk about race and racism in the City is dangerously simplistic. I was hired in part *because* I talked about race and racism in the City and continued to do so despite several tense encounters. Committees are formed in the City specifically to talk about racism. The City hosts many consultations with Toronto residents on how it can do better at addressing racism in its midst. Racialized staff are also hired in the City, particularly in the People, Equity & Human Rights Division (formerly Equity, Diversity & Human Rights, and before that, Access, Equity & Human Rights) because of their "expertise" in racial issues. In fact, they contribute significantly to the City's diversity narrative, not just in terms of the racial representation they bring, but also because of what they *do* in and for the City to tackle racism and discrimination. This, I argue, is why we need to pay close attention to how and under what terms race and racism in the City are discussed, and by whom.

Exceptional via the "Outside"

The common thread that ran throughout all of my interviews with racialized City staff was that they needed to justify their belonging in the City. Whether staff were more progressive than most, or had the "right" language, or were going to be "the one" to finally do diversity differently, or didn't see race, or didn't need to rely on race/claims of racism to get their positions or to be good at their jobs, they belonged in the City because they were exceptional – in many respects "better" than most Others at thinking through diversity. And yet these exceptional subjectivities were premised on and accessed through racial norms that reproduce a racial outside(r). The argument I have begun to carefully sketch out in this chapter and will continue to build throughout the rest of the book is that subjectivity and belonging for the racial insider are authorized (though not necessarily *granted*) through the reproduction of this outside(r).

Before I conclude this chapter, I want to spend a bit of time focusing on how the City also *pulls* the outside(r) – as the site(s) of race/racism – into its reproduction as exceptional. There are several examples in City texts. For example, in May 1994, Toronto City Council rescinded its economic sanctions against South Africa as a result of its "ending [of] 46 years of constitutionalized apartheid" (City of Toronto, 1994). The motion to Council to rescind economic sanctions congratulates the African National Congress and the South African government for "the progress being made toward racial harmony and democracy" (p. 1813) and then explicitly states, in a number of places and in a number of ways, the City of Toronto's role in making the end of apartheid in South Africa possible:

> Further be it resolved that City Council, *in acknowledging of the significant role its policies and advocacy for disinvestment in South Africa have played in the bringing down apartheid through economic sanctions*, recognize its continued responsibility to support South Africa in the process of achieving its goals as a peaceful, non-racial, non-sexist, economically viable democratic nation where all of its citizenry are empowered to achieve their aspirations for food, clean water, housing, health, education, employment, and culture. (p. 1812; my emphasis)

In this text, the City is also presented as a role model for South Africa, specifically through positioning the exceptionally progressive and healthy state of the City against the exceptionally desolate state of South Africa:

> [I]n conjunction with the Federal Government, [the City of Toronto] could offer to share with South African municipalities their municipal government expertise, particularly in the areas of public health, housing, and public works so that South Africa achieves its goals of providing good health for all its citizenry and housing for the more than 10 million Black South Africans who live in squatter camps or unsafe, inadequate, overcrowded conditions without benefit of basic services. (p. 1813)

The City's *Supplementary Report: 2011 Progress Report on Equity, Diversity and Human Rights Achievements* (City of Toronto, 2012b) draws on and recirculates familiar "celebratory" diversity rhetoric:

> Toronto welcomes the cosmopolitan diversity from immigration. It brings with it tremendous cultural richness and cross-cultural knowledge. From street names, heritage architecture, cultural celebrations to art, music, literature and sports, the diversity created by immigrants and refugees has enriched the quality of life for all. (p. 8)

And then, "*It is remarkable that Toronto is free from the social tension and conflict that trouble some American and European cities*" (p. 8; my emphasis).

The October 2013 *Notice of Motion: Reaffirming Toronto's Strong Support for Freedom of Religion and Expression* (City of Toronto, 2013) put forward by Councillor James Pasternak and seconded by Councillor Joe Mihevc, pulls in the Government of Quebec's proposal for legislation that would prohibit public employees from wearing visible religious symbols in the workplace, only to "assure residents and visitors to Toronto that our City will always welcome people of all faiths, and protect their freedom of religion and expression," "as one of the world's most diverse cities, and in keeping with our motto 'Diversity Our Strength'" (p. 1). The motion makes only one recommendation:

> That City Council reaffirm its support for freedom of religion and expression, and, further state its opposition to any legislation that would restrict or prohibit such freedoms. By doing so, Toronto states its position that the City continues to be a source of worldwide inspiration. (p. 1)

The irony in these examples, as in several others, is that the City needn't actually do anything about racism in the City to be exceptional for addressing racism. In this, race and racism are expelled *and expendable*; the diverse City can at any point draw on and then reproduce the outside(r) to suture its own spatial and racial anxieties, triggered by increasing encounters unmanageable by diversity. But if what Razack (2002) says is true, that bodies produce space and space produces bodies, we might need to concern ourselves with how the exceptionally diverse City invites, produces, and co-authorizes the exceptional racial subject to draw on the outside(r) as well, to reassure their anxieties of belonging in a space that would otherwise not have them.

On Diversity and Racial Inclusion

In interviews, we never fully arrived at the question of *why* racialized City staff needed to be exceptional in the City or why they felt they needed to set themselves apart. Indeed, this is the power (and precisely the point) of the production of subjectivity: its hailing and engendering of individualities and potential meeting of desires obscures or even *invalidates* deeper questions centred upon how race and power might continue to manifest through us. But perhaps more importantly, the need for racial insiders to be exceptional in the City also speaks volumes about the space of the diverse City; more specifically, who belongs there as well as why and the terms under which racial Others are "included."

In this regard, we as racial insider Others must ask ourselves what we are doing *for* diversity. Of course, this question is not new. But research and scholarship on diversity, equity, and inclusion (including the growing body of research and scholarship on racism and racialization) still tend to focus on how racism and whiteness are maintained in institutions through racial exclusion (see Henry et al., 2017, p. 300, for list of scholars who write about this). One of my aims in this chapter is to get us thinking about how, in the age of diversity, racism and whiteness in institutions are maintained and increasingly authorized through racial *inclusion*. This is perhaps the most central paradox for racialized City staff who take up the position of being exceptionally critical of diversity in the City of Toronto: they are produced, included, and authorized in the City through the very racial terms they seek to challenge.

That being said, the terms of inclusion for racial insider Others in the City are anything but seamless. As I have begun to show, moments of tension in speech acts and in City texts expose the anxieties of racial inclusion and belonging in the diverse City and also bring into question the production and psychic separation(s) of "us" and "them" that diversity seeks to guarantee through the production and inclusion of exceptional racial insider Others in particular. Through racial inclusion, the racial norms of diversity discourse in the City thus also become unstable. The instabilities are what drive this book. The next chapter continues to trace the instabilities and anxieties of diversity discourse, this time through the production, inclusion, and proximity of racial Others like no Other in the diverse City.

Chapter Four

Being Like No Other:
Building Inside(r) Relations Through Race

On 30 June 1993, the Toronto Mayor's Committee on Community and Race Relations put forward a motion recommending that Toronto City Council congratulate the more than 80 anti-racist organizations for organizing an orderly, successful, and peaceful anti-racist demonstration held on 28 June of that same year. For the Mayor's Committee, the demonstration was "proof that the Coalition of Anti-Racist Organizations has reclaimed the advantage in its efforts to fight white supremacist racist organizations" (City of Toronto, 1993b, p. 10). In the motion, there is specific reference to the success and reclaimed advantage of the demonstration being attributed to organizers establishing "a good liaison with the Metropolitan Toronto Police" (p. 10).

The commendation given to the anti-racist demonstration and its organizers is the only one of its kind in the City's history and is both perplexing and rather ill-placed. Several government and media reports were released just prior, pointing to institutionalized racism in Toronto policing. In early 1992 the Metro Toronto Police Services Board initiated a study on racial bias in the collection of crime statistics following a series of controversial statements from high-ranking police and other City officials on the problems of what they called "black crime" and "Asian crime" in Toronto (City of Toronto, 1992a, p. 7; Jackson, 1994). The May 1992 Yonge Street riot in solidarity with Rodney King and in response to the police shooting death of yet another Black man in Toronto spawned an official race relations audit of Metro police (Jackson, 1994). The audit later revealed strong evidence that Toronto police officers developed racializing ideas and stereotypes once they joined the force, which led to racial bias and discrimination on and off duty (Andrews, 1992). The City was also facing an overwhelming number of complaints regarding the racial profiling of Black men (Roach, 1999). In all of this, the Toronto Mayor's Committee on Community and Race

Relations was given the task of increasing "understanding and dialogue between the Police and the City's diverse communities" (City of Toronto, 1991a, p. 12). In light of the "crisis in relations" between them, the Committee made it their mission "to restore mutual respect and trust between the Black community and the police" (City of Toronto, 1991b, p. 204).

So why take the time and effort to single out and congratulate this particular anti-racist demonstration? At its core, the motion from the Toronto Mayor's Committee draws on and reproduces the racial norms of diversity discourse to maintain racial and spatial innocence. Implicit in singling out the anti-racism demonstration as peaceful, orderly, and successful is the assumption that anti-racists, anti-racist action, and claims of racism in the diverse City typically *lack* these characteristics. As I began to articulate in the previous chapter, racial lack is grounded in colonial, racial, and normative thinking and is both constitutive and an effect of diversity discourse in the City of Toronto. In addition, the motion documented that for the over 80 anti-racist organizations and the "more than 2,000 anti-racists of all colours" (p. 10) who participated in the demonstration, the real racist threats in Toronto were not Metro police but the growing number of well-organized right-wing hate propagandists, including pro-Nazi apologist Ernst Zundel[1] and the Ku Klux Klan. The motion not only served to reproduce the City as a not-racist space, it set up and perhaps even deferred claims of racism in the City against the spectres of Nazism and white hoods.

For the Toronto Mayor's Committee, however, the anti-racist organizers and demonstrators were worthy of special attention because of their positive relationship with Metro police. That this relationship was singled out politically and institutionally through City texts only increased its significance. Amidst rising claims of police racism and increasing tensions between police and the city's racialized communities, the motion from the Toronto Mayor's Committee conveyed the sense that over 80 anti-racist organizations as well as thousands of anti-racist demonstrators from across the city put whatever grievances they may have had with Metro police aside to leverage their fight against racism in Toronto. This is what made organizers and demonstrators a special kind of anti-racist in the City.

The motion from the Toronto Mayor's Committee both anchors and introduces the central argument of this chapter: racial Others are invited and produced, through the racial norms of diversity discourse, to be like no racial Other in the City of Toronto. As I discovered through research for this book, being like no Other in the City of Toronto is not a unique phenomenon. For almost four decades, select racial Others have been specially recognized and included in the City of Toronto, through City texts and in speech acts, for being "not like them" – racial other Others who are abjected in the City for being race(d). As I will show, in being like no Other, racial Others gain varying degrees of trust with and proximity to the white, male, middle-class somatic norm.

In *On Being Included*, Ahmed (2012) offers a brief but very insightful account of the pressure on people of colour in diverse institutions to be the "right kind" of minority (p. 158). In the happy image of diversity, bodies of colour are expected to be the difference that diversity requires but to never *assert* that difference. The hyper-surveillance of difference in diverse institutions often results in people of colour engaging in careful modes of self-presentation, in particular a deliberate distancing from the racializing ideas and stereotypes that are imposed upon bodies who appear to pose a problem or who are out of place.[2] Ahmed concludes that diversity makes speaking about racism deliberately dangerous for people of colour, if not impossible.

Following Ahmed, I would agree that the exceptional subjectivities of the anti-racist demonstrators I referred to earlier are articulated through a distancing from the "problem" of institutionalized racism in the City as well as those who take it up. However, what I found most compelling in the motion, as I did in several other City texts as well as interview transcripts, is that trust, proximity, and belonging for racial Others like no Other in the City of Toronto is further garnered through their inclusion in institutionalized processes of (re-)producing racializing ideas and stereotypes elsewhere, outside the bounds of the diverse City. This, I argue, is one of the ways race is reproduced through diversity discourse in the specific, local context that is the City of Toronto – being like no Other requires uncivilized racial other Others outside of the diverse City, as the sites of race.

This chapter seeks to explicate what remains largely unseen. Drawing on City texts and interview transcripts, my aim is to show that reproducing racialization and sites of race outside the diverse City is a deeply embedded, conditioned, and institutionalized practice of building trust, proximity, and belonging for racial Others like no Other. In sections one and two, I discuss City texts that emanate from and are produced through two "events"[3] in the City of Toronto's history – the establishment of the Toronto Mayor's Committee on Community and Race Relations (1980) and the position of the Diversity Advocate on Council (2000). I explore these "events" as paradigmatic of the institutionalization of trust, proximity, and belonging for racial Others like no Other in the City of Toronto. In the third section, I describe how racialized City staff draw on stereotypes and "specialized knowledge" of racial other Others to bolster their belonging as like no Other in the City. I show how distancing themselves ("us") from racial other Others ("them") brings racialized City staff in closer proximity to the somatic norm, making them more trustworthy racial subjects.

In the fourth section, I return to City texts to demonstrate that, even in attempts to address or challenge stereotypes, the City reinforces the essentialization and racialization of bodies, naturalizes the somatic norm in the space of the City, and re-confirms the space of the City as like no Other and innocent. Finally, I consider how the historical, institutionalized racial norms and practices of "being like no Other" carry into the reproductions of diversity and race in the current political moment. I also illuminate and reflect on some of the paradoxes of psychic investments in and desires to be like no Other, particularly when invited and produced through diversity discourse in the City of Toronto.

Although the institutional recognition of "special" racial Others in the City of Toronto might at first glance appear arbitrary, in this chapter I trace how their activations manifest and re-authorize specific, local, and historical "truths" about diversity, race, and power. In doing so, I also make the case that the production and differential inclusion of racial Others like no Other in the diverse City is always-already set up to further naturalize the somatic norm and the space of the City as innocent.

Anti-racism Like No Other

The process of building trust, proximity, and belonging through racialization was particularly evident when, in December 1980, former Toronto Mayor Art Eggleton established the Toronto Mayor's Committee on Community and Race Relations. The Committee's twelve members, "picked on the basis of their knowledge of and commitment to fighting racial discrimination," were charged with helping the City to "root out racism as much as possible" (City of Toronto, 1981b, p. 8077). As Mayor Eggleton explained, the priorities of the Committee were to address the increased presence of white supremacist organizations in Toronto, the onslaught of Ontario Human Rights complaints about racism, and fraught relations between police and visible minority communities (City of Toronto, 1981a). The Committee was also directed to give advice to the City on "employment opportunities for minorities at City Hall and other municipal agencies" (City of Toronto, 1980b, p. 359). It is worth noting here that for Mayor Eggleton initially, the underemployment of visible minorities in the City and racism were two separate issues. However, in the final report explaining the justification for the Committee, Mayor Eggleton described why diversifying the City's workforce was linked to combating racism in Toronto:

> As the old saying goes, "Charity begins at home," and our own house must be in good order if we are to effectively solicit public support in the struggle against prejudice and discrimination. I believe that the Committee on Community and Race Relations can assist in this endeavour by working with us to make the City of Toronto a model employer, undertaking whatever programs are necessary to sharpen our responsiveness to the employment needs of minority communities. (City of Toronto, 1981a, p. 1054)

As I have argued, the under-representation of racialized bodies in the City is repeatedly co-articulated with "their" lack of skills, knowledge, and experience, in order to maintain the City as a diverse, exceptional, and innocent space. However, in this final justification for the Mayor's Committee, addressing under-representation also gets taken up as the charity work of the City. The reframing of racial exclusion as charity work reproduces colonial relationships where those who are entrusted with power and civility are infused with the moral sensibilities to save uncivilized racial (other) Others. As Goldberg (1993) brilliantly explains, the historical construction of the white male subject as racially superior is largely accomplished and sustained "by constituting racial others outside the scope of morality" (p. 39). In addition, appealing to the good, moral intentions and desires of the bourgeois white male subject to help racial Others reproduces and obscures his rightful place and racial superiority in the City, as one who is "naturally" more evolved, skilled, knowledgeable, and moral, but also innocent of racism. Ultimately, the turn toward the language of morality is embedded in the same discourses of racial lack, to further naturalize the somatic norm and his innocence in the City.

Yet in an interesting twist, the racialized members of the Toronto Mayor's Committee were authorized to "root out racism" through these same moral terms. Mayor Eggleton suggested the Committee could help "diverse groups" in how they talked about racism:

> It is my hope that the Committee on Community and Race Relations will strive to increase the ability of diverse groups to communicate and interact effectively in eradicating racism and prejudice from within our midst. Serving as a "Broker" between conflicting groups, it will help improve inter-group relations in Toronto. (City of Toronto, 1981a, p. 1055)

In this official introduction of the Committee as a body that would increase the abilities of "diverse groups," racialized Committee members were pre-emptively ordained as like no Other in the diverse City, in racial terms. Select racial Others were invited and produced as Committee members under the terms that they had transgressed the limits of racial lack, which continued to impede the ability of outside "diverse groups" to communicate and interact effectively in the City on issues of racism. Addressing claims of racism in the City thus became formally institutionalized and streamlined through a process that relied on and reproduced separations between "us," racial insider Others like no Other, and "them," abjected other Others as the sites of race. In addition, as more skilled, knowledgeable, and effective racial Others now endowed with the moral obligation of helping racial other Others address their claims, racialized Committee members were more closely aligned with the somatic norm in the diverse City. Perhaps what is most crucial to consider is that racialized Committee members were produced and became articulate(d) in closer proximity to the somatic norm – as moral subjects who help uncivilized other Others – to ensure that they would not draw attention to their own bodies as raced, or more specifically, to not make their own claims of racism. The proximity and trustworthiness of racialized Committee members like no Other in the diverse City thus relied on the continuity of race but also the threat of its visibility when negotiating the axes of belonging and subjectivity, as racial insider Others in the diverse City.

Civility in the City

Although the production of racialized Committee members as moral subjects may have inhibited their own claims of racism, outside "diverse groups" continued to bring theirs to the table. And with the formalization of the Mayor's Committee, addressing racism in the City appeared to be at the top of the City's agenda. But as Mayo (2002) reminds us, civility – the historical practice of maintaining social interaction, recognition, tolerance, and respect – is premised on the capacity of social actors to repress their "private" grievances that would otherwise disrupt social and political spheres. This not only limits what discussions can take place, but who participates and how – those who complain about racism, for example, are deemed uncivil because they lack the ability to repress their anger for the good of civil society.[4] And in "diverse" societies of today, "if civility requires leaving unspoken things that would disturb placid social interactions, the practice of civility will necessarily leave out those whose presence disrupts the bias that presumes their absence" (p. 174).[5]

Under the terms of civility, we can begin to make sense of how and why racial other Others continued to be left out: their claims of institutionalized racism in policing and in other areas of the City disrupted the diverse City's narrative of racial innocence, which presumed the absence of their racial claims. But if discussing racism in social and political spheres circumvents the parameters of civility and therefore should remain private, why propose a formal Committee of the City and invite racialized members whose task it was to discuss racism? Did the presence of the Committee itself not disrupt the bias of the City as tolerant, welcoming, respectful, and diverse?

To answer these questions, we need to think about *how and why* the Committee talked about racism in the City. I proposed earlier that by racialized Committee members drawing attention to their own bodies as raced, including through speaking about racism, they would have transgressed their trustworthiness, proximity, belonging, and subjectivities as like no Other in the diverse City. However, given their responsibilities of restoring respect and trust between Toronto police and the City's diverse communities, being brokers between conflicting groups and helping "diverse groups" to effectively address their claims of racism in the diverse City, what I also propose is that the racialized members of the Toronto Mayor's Committee were produced to have a regulatory effect on "outsider" claims of police and other forms of institutionalized racism in the diverse City, as well as how they were taken up. In other words, I am suggesting that the racialized members of the Toronto Mayor's Committee on Community and Race Relations were invited, produced, and authorized like no Other in the diverse City, as *civilizing racial subjects*.

For example, in 1984 the Toronto Mayor's Committee held community consultations in response to hearing "problems that members of ethnic and racial minorities had encountered in getting access to municipal services" (City of Toronto, 1990a, p. 152). Although the "problems" identified by minorities included racial barriers in the City,[6] the community consultation process was organized with a specific focus on inviting "newer immigrants who, *because of their cultural and language backgrounds*, had difficulty in getting adequate access to services" (p. 152; my emphasis). In fact, the Toronto Mayor's Committee chose to hold consultations "by ethnic group" (p. 153).[7] Here, issues of racism in the City get reframed by assigning ethnic groups – *all of whom are racialized* – a lack of cultural integration and language skills.[8] It was through the reproduction of these racializing norms that Mayor Eggleton could begin the final report consolidating issues brought forward in the consultations, including issues of racism, with the following statement:

> The City has approved statements of equal opportunity believing them to be an accurate reflection of the character of the people of Toronto. They help define the City as a successful, cosmopolitan centre, where a diversity of people can live and work together in harmony. (City of Toronto, 1990b, p. 1290)

On 27 October 1988, the Toronto Mayor's Committee also recommended, in keeping with its mandate "to promote understanding and respect among racial, cultural, ethnic and religious community groups in the City" (City of Toronto, 1989b, p. 111), that 1989 be designated as the Year of Racial Harmony. The Committee organized a year-long program of special events "celebrating Toronto's ethnic and cultural diversity" (City of Toronto, 1989a, p. 1309), which included inviting schools across Toronto to participate in essay, poetry, photography, dramatic performance, and art contests to capture the racially harmonious character of the city, under the banner "Together We Are Toronto" (City of Toronto, 1989b, p. 111). Importantly, the Committee's proposal and planning for the Year of Racial Harmony coincided with a series of police shootings involving Toronto's Black community and a rapid decline in police-community relations (Jackson, 1994).

Produced as civilizing racial subjects, racialized Committee members served as gatekeepers for how, where, and with whom racism in the City was discussed – a role that the white male somatic norm could no longer fulfil alone, especially in a City becoming widely known for its commitments to diversity and equal opportunity. Importantly, several other Committee initiatives either addressed racism outside of the City or requested that others outside the City take action where the City already had, in effect further reproducing the somatic norm and reinforcing the idea of the City as innocent. And, as evidenced in City texts, the more the Mayor's Committee institutionalized civility in racial terms that marked the City as innocent, the more trust, support, and credibility they gained.[9] While thousands of anti-racist demonstrators were produced like no Other against other Others in the 1993 motion, so too were the racialized members of the Toronto Mayor's Committee, through the very act of putting the motion forward. In further institutionalizing the historical practices of "leaving out" uncivil, untrustworthy racial other Others who disrupted the bias of the diverse City with their claims of racism, racialized Committee members became more trustworthy racial insider Others, in closer proximity to the somatic norm and ultimately re-authorized as like no Other.

This is not to say that the Toronto Mayor's Committee on Community and Race Relations did not attempt to subvert the racial binds of civility and diversity. As I described in the previous chapter, the Mayor's Committee submitted a report for the 1986–90 Equal Opportunity Program Review, which stated that "salaries among racial minorities in the civic workforce have been declining relative to whites" (p. 75), and that "Native people" and racial minorities were still significantly under-represented in the City's workforce, despite the City's claims of equal opportunity. In this, the Mayor's Committee simultaneously identified ongoing racism in the City and initiated a framing of equal opportunity as a discourse in the City.

On 27 March 1991, the Committee advised City Council that they were rejecting Council's previously adopted motion commending Police Chief William McCormack for his "balanced, responsive and sensitive leadership" on race relations and cultural sensitivity programs (City of Toronto, 1991c, p. 158). On 7 December 1992, City Council passed a motion to "express its outrage" (City of Toronto, 1992c, p. 19) at a series of racist activities in the city and to also congratulate the Metropolitan Toronto Police Force for establishing a hate crimes unit, as part of their larger strategy to combat racist hate in Toronto. Subsequently, on 27 January 1993, the Toronto Mayor's Committee acknowledged that although Metro police's hate crime unit was "a step in the right direction" (City of Toronto, 1993a, p. 40), the City's enthusiasm towards it precluded an acknowledgment of the serious lack of in-depth resources, expertise, or training required for police to properly address racist hate crimes.

Although these and other subversive acts from the Committee were inevitably reframed or disregarded altogether via the reproduction of racial norms, in each of their moments they exposed the larger anxieties and ruptures of inviting, producing, and including racial Others like no Other in the diverse City. What they reveal is that the production of racial subjectivities in the diverse City can never finally, fully be foreclosed as long as racial difference in the diverse City is experienced and denied. If being like no Other in the diverse City adds up to transgressing of the limits of one's race to warrant inclusion, that inclusion should not still be experienced differentially. And yet, because of race, it is. Even the incorporation of the Toronto Mayor's Committee, as an advisory body with no decision-making power, betrayed the promise of full subjectivity and belonging in the City. For those who are produced to be like no Other, the danger of fully corroborating with diversity discourse and the denial of race is the inevitable effacement of their own embodied experiences of being no more than the difference that diversity and the space of the City require.

The risk of racial inclusion in diverse institutions, to return to a point so eloquently stated by both Ahmed and Puwar, is that it requires racial Others to be complicit with being the desired difference of diversity, without naming that difference. Naming race exposes the invisibility, normativity, but also *fallibility* of whiteness in discourses of diversity, equal opportunity, equity, inclusion, intersectionality, progress, democracy, and so on. However, in the specific and local context of the City of Toronto, the power of subversive acts is that they additionally render re-significations of a civilized "us" and an uncivilized "them" (which make up and reproduce the diverse and innocent City) completely unreliable and unpredictable.

Still, I would argue that the inclusion of select "resistant" racial Others can also further facilitate discursive and spatial containment, to re-present resistance as examples of both the limitlessness of the City's racial inclusion paradigm and the absolute flexibility and *permeability* of the space. In this, the various issues associated with assigning the task of addressing City-wide issues of racism to *one* committee, again, with no power to generate policy or action, become obscured. In fact, no committee formed to address racism in the City of Toronto has ever had any real decision-making power.[10] We might consider, then, how the formation of various committees specifically to address racism is in itself meant to *silo* and, by extension, disarm larger racial resistances and demands for action in the City, as I began to articulate in the previous chapter. Resistance moves provoke anxieties in the already delicate balance of war and constraint that underpin diversity's remaking in the present. The question to consider here, again, is how these anxieties might be recovered through the very idea of (or desire for) an exceptional space, position, and/or subjectivity in the City.

Diversity Like No Other

On 5 December 2000 City Council passed a motion establishing the City of Toronto's first and only Diversity Advocate position, a role fulfilled by former City Councillor Sherene Shaw. As Diversity Advocate, Councillor Shaw was to "act as the City's primary spokesperson and advocate on diversity issues," help reflect the City's motto "Diversity Our Strength," "promote, support and enhance Toronto's position on Diversity, and Access and Equity strategies, both locally, nationally, and internationally" (City of Toronto, 2000b, p. 23), and show support for the elimination of violence, racism, and all barriers to human rights. To fulfil these tasks, the City's Chief Administrative Officer (CAO) recommended that Councillor Shaw be responsible for consulting with the five City-wide Advisory Committees on Access and Equity (Aboriginal Affairs, Disability Issues, Status of Women, Race and Ethnic Relations, and Lesbian, Gay, Bisexual, and Transgender Issues), community organizations, groups, and Toronto residents on issues of diversity to create a consolidated *Diversity Advocate Action Plan* (City of Toronto, 2001b). The CAO also recommended that Councillor Shaw "work with staff on specific initiatives in the Council Action Plan, such as the mentoring program for foreign trained professionals; strategies for building the economic capacity of communities; and responding to planning and regulatory issues regarding places of worship for the City's diverse communities" (City of Toronto, 2001b, p. 2).

Councillor Shaw responded to these recommendations in her final Diversity Advocate Action Plan report:

As the Diversity Advocate, I have reviewed the CAO's report and am in concurrence with the proposed approach. This approach builds upon the existing structure established by City Council and can provide a mechanism for co-coordinating issues across the various advisory committees and our diverse communities in Toronto. (City of Toronto, 2001b, p. 3)

The Diversity Advocate's consultation strategy and consolidated plan was also effective because, in the words of Councillor Shaw, they would eliminate "an overlap in common issues" (City of Toronto, 2001b, p. 3) and continue the City's diversity work at no extra cost to the City.

As the only racialized woman City Councillor and as a member of the Status of Women Community Advisory Committee, Councillor Shaw was arguably already embroiled in institutionalized processes of building trust, proximity, and belonging through racialization. As such, Councillor Shaw's production as Diversity Advocate and as like no Other was to some degree institutionally and politically "pre-authorized." Building trust and proximity through racialization was also exemplified through Councillor Shaw's concurrence that her responsibilities as Diversity Advocate should include working with City staff to further mentoring programs and build the economic capacities of "diverse" communities. Although framed as a commitment to eliminate all forms of racism and discrimination in the City, as I have shown, mentoring programs and building "their" capacities historically and specifically attaches an essence of lack to racial other Others in the diverse City.

Significantly, however, the City's CAO gave Councillor Shaw the numerous responsibilities of the Diversity Advocate under the explicit terms that they "enhance the access and equity initiatives already approved by Council in December 1999" (City of Toronto, 2001a, p. 2). These initiatives, 97 in total, arose from over two years of consultation sessions and extensive cross-sector research lead by the City's Task Force on Community Access and Equity, a group of 18 brought together to ensure that access and equity for the City's most marginalized groups remained a top priority in the newly amalgamated City. The 97 initiatives also formed the basis of the final Action Plan of the City of Toronto Task Force on Community Access and Equity (City of Toronto, 1999c).

So why create a new Diversity Advocate position and Action Plan to address access and equity in the City, if they were to just reiterate or maybe slightly enhance what the City's Task Force on Access and Equity had finalized just one year earlier? Under what terms can we consider Councillor Shaw to have been produced differently, as like no Other, in her role as Diversity Advocate in the City? If we borrow the logic of civility described above, we can see how Councillor Shaw was produced as the City's Diversity Advocate to police the terms of civility with community groups and Toronto residents who might bring their experiences of racism to the newly amalgamated City. However, it is also important to note here that the recommendations of the Task Force on Community Access and Equity included the creation of five new City-wide Advisory Committees, each made up of 18 citizen members and one member of Council. Each Committee was given the task of facilitating communication on and addressing community concerns, specifically barriers to access, equity, and human rights in the diverse City. The five Committees were also to closely monitor and give feedback on the City's progress on creating inclusive community participation in all aspects of City life (City of Toronto, 1999c).

With at least two of the five Committees having the potential to focus on racism in the City[11] I suggest that, as with the racialized members of the Toronto Mayor's Committee on Community and Race Relations, the production of Councillor Shaw as the Diversity Advocate and as like no Other was in response to race being too close. Although the circumstances for each "production" were unique – the racialized members of the Toronto Mayor's Committee during increasing claims of police racism and the City's Diversity Advocate following the mass institutionalization of "outsider" claims-making – in both cases there was great risk of undoing the narrative of the diverse City. If, as Diversity Advocate, Councillor Shaw was to act as a spokesperson for the five Advisory

Committees, local community groups, and Toronto residents who had concerns about barriers to access and equity in the City, it is certainly worth considering that she was produced as like no Other to strictly reinforce the terms of civility and thus to abject racial other Others as the sites of race, in and across multiple sites.

In fact, the abjection of racial other Others drove both the process and content of the City of Toronto's (2003a) *Plan of Action for the Elimination of Racism and Discrimination*, led by Councillor Shaw in her role as Diversity Advocate. Without question, continuing to abject race and racism in a widely publicized plan specifically seeking to combat racism in the City would have been a difficult task, particularly when multiple advisory and stakeholder groups, community organizations, activists, and City residents were expressly invited to talk about their racist experiences. But as Ahmed (2000) reminds us in her work on multiculturalism discourse in Australia, the multicultural nation also reinvents itself through "refusing any differences that cannot be contained within the discourses of individualism or the unified nation" (p. 103). Those who belong in the nation are hailed into national subject-positions against the "unassimilable" figure of the stranger stranger who is incorporated in the multicultural nation as its limit – what "we" cannot and will not be.

On the whole, I agree with Ahmed's argument that the figure of stranger stranger (whom I term the racial other Other/outsider) embodies and is incorporated as the limit of racial discourses such as multiculturalism and diversity. However, in this book I hope to underscore a slightly different argument: those who embody the limits of diversity in the City of Toronto – racial other Others and their claims of racism – are repeatedly, methodically invited into the City because their abjection is necessary to the reproduction of diversity discourse and the various racial subjectivities that are produced through it. In this, we might consider how the positioning of the Diversity Advocate and others like no Other would not have been produced if it were not for experiences of racism in the diverse City, which remarkably, through repeated abjection and erasure, remain largely unaddressed.

I want to close this section by offering my reflections on a small excerpt in Kristin Good's *Municipalities and Multiculturalism* that details her interview with Toronto City Councillor Joe Mihevc on the topic of the Diversity Advocate. Good writes that, according to Councillor Mihevc, "the Diversity Advocate can be effective only if a councillor with the ability to lead on these issues is appointed to the role" (p. 61). In Councillor Mihevc's view, Councillor Shaw's appointment to the role of Diversity Advocate by then-Mayor Mel Lastman was a strategic move; a deliberate attempt to limit progress on access and equity in the City.

Notwithstanding the critiques we might have of a white male City Councillor taking issue with the only racialized woman on Council leading the City's diversity work, once again there is the idea that one can "do" diversity differently. This is the point I think Councillor Mihevc is trying to make: with his history of leading access and equity initiatives in the City, if he was appointed Diversity Advocate, he could have done diversity better. As I argued in the previous chapter, the idea that one can "do" diversity differently or better is actually an effect of diversity discourse, race, and power and is also integral to their continuities in the present.[12] But more than this, the claim that Councillor Shaw did not have the ability to lead on issues of diversity assumes a particular performance of diversity work in the City that Councillor Shaw could not, even as a "diverse" body herself, fulfil. Through his assertion, Councillor Mihevc further naturalizes the white male somatic norm as one who knows how to "do" diversity and effectively reproduces terms under which racial Others become trustworthy and capable in the diverse City: *through proximity.*

Invoking the Stereotype

Bhabha (1994) contends that the function of the stereotype is to fix the Other as an object and as inferior, in racial terms. However, the need for constant repetition of the stereotype questions the very fixity that the repetition sets out to guarantee. In Bhabha's view, the repetition of the stereotype contains the anxiety and dependency of the colonizer's identity on the reproduction of its colonized Other – what he calls "productive ambivalence" (p. 67).

To further unsettle the fixity of the stereotype, Bhabha theorizes the role of hybridity in the in-between "third space of enunciation" (p. 56). In this third space, the anxieties of the colonizer meet the colonized Other's negotiations, performances, and contestations of identity *in excess of* fixity and colonial binaries, creating the possibility for "new signs of identity, and innovative sites of collaboration, and contestation, in the act of defining the idea of society itself" (p. 1). For Bhabha, the third space is where the colonized find the potential for agency and the destabilization of the colonial, essentialist narratives and discourses that justify racial superiority and racial violence.

In interviews, racialized City staff invoked racial stereotypes to distance themselves from essentialized racial characteristics and ideas. Drawing on Bhabha's notion of hybridity, one might argue that this distancing from racial stereotypes is an attempt to open up a third space, in excess of racial representations of identity. However, in carefully tracing the terms under which the racial stereotype is evoked by staff, I seek to underline that their desires for "new" not-raced identities are confined by and produced through the historical, racial norms of diversity discourse in the City of Toronto, under the guise that being like no Other *is a third space of enunciation*. In this vein, I respectfully question Bhahba's insistence that hybridity in the third space moves beyond traditionalist, essentialist discourses to "entertain difference without an assumed or imposed hierarchy" (p. 5). Instead, I hope to make visible that the positionings staff take up that are purportedly outside of colonial, racial signifiers ignite in diversity discourse what Rose (1996) calls "the invention of new regimes of subjectification" (p. 141), to reproduce historical, racial knowledges and truths in the present, in the world and in how we come to view ourselves.

For example, although Corey in some ways feels that he is being used to provide "good visual optics" in diverse hiring in the City, he also explained that he uses his position "as a positive example ... who was given an opportunity" to be a leader for racialized communities:

> I'm leading in terms of [*long pause*] let's go. Come. This is where I was, let me tell you what I used to do and how I got here. And when I go to different communities, I have no qualms about telling them, I grew up in similar ... because, when they see me represent the different ... optically, I present a different thing to them. Because now my, my pants not baggy, my boots are not, shoes are not tucked into my boots, my clothes are not tucked into my boot. So this is who I am now.

Corey also believes that showing people from racialized communities that he is not "a father with a baby mama" inspires people from racialized communities to believe that "it doesn't have to be that way" for them, either.

Kevin also described his leadership in the City as a staff person of colour who "knows these communities." Recalling a multi-departmental project he was a part of, Kevin explained some of the frustrations he had with moving it forward in a way that had genuine concern for the needs of the community, beyond the City's typical "diversity actions, because their action out there is translators." For Kevin, real diversity work included him mentoring a white staff person on how to build trust with the mostly racialized residents affected by the project:

> I told him, "Don't ever wear a suit and tie, 'cause you look like a law-yer. Do you know what I mean? Like, first and, like, very first principles, very simple things. Or, you know, don't do PowerPoint presentations, sit amongst ... do you know what I mean?

These difficulties also led Kevin to think about pursuing an area of study to learn how to train white staff on how "to govern yourself as a [department position], when you're communicating with people of, you know, different ... races? Races, I don't ... races. I hate, I don't like that word."

Kevin and Corey's accounts reflect an underlying thread that ran through each interview I conducted: staff needed to explicitly justify their positions as racial insider Others in the City. Their modes of justi-fication suggest that occupying space as racialized staff feels unnatural and tenuous – for some, even after a decade or more in the City. Racial stereotypes in particular were drawn on so staff could articulate that they exceeded them – unlike racial other Others outside the diverse City – *which is how and why they became staff*. They also spoke of their specialized, "insider" knowledge of racialized communities that would help the City to more authentically serve community needs – a point I will return to later. As self-proclaimed leaders, experts, and facilitators, staff moved in closer proximity to the somatic norm but also in excess of ideological, essentializing prescriptions of their identities as raced. In other words, "not quite white" (Bhabha, 1994, p. 89) but also not like "them."

Yet in my reading of interview transcripts against City of Toronto texts, I began to notice remarkable similarities between the ways staff articulated their identities in excess of race and institutionalized pro-cesses of building trust, proximity, and belonging as like no Other in the diverse City. My comparative reading also produced a series of ques-tions involving Bhabha's work. If racial Others seek a third space where they transgress monolithic racial identities and hegemonic narratives, against what racial identities is this space accessed? Can we truly con-sider hybrid subjectivity in the third space an "insurgent act of cultural translation" (p. 10), as Bhabha would suggest, if in this space one turns away from prescriptive identities of the racial Other – "I am not this/ them" – in effect reproducing these very prescriptions? Can hybrid sub-jectivities in the third space be desired and sustained independently of the historical discursive and material effects of race and not-belonging?

While a full discussion on the possibilities and limitations of Bhabha's third space is beyond the scope of this chapter, my reading of interview transcripts against City texts led me to a point of interrogating whether the insurgent act was in the third space itself or an illumination of its modes of production and articulation, in relations of power.

Although she had no illusions that she alone could change the way the City thinks about diversity, Nicole explained that her "legitimacy," "credibility in the community," and "know[ing] what the community issues are" helps her to be taken seriously when she pushes the City to develop an analysis on "how within diversity also there's privilege and marginality." In our interview, Nicole used herself as an example to describe differential access in society that the City's diversity work had yet to capture:

> The way I dressed, my body language, the way I talked, the idioms ...
> I'm much more accessible to their image of themselves [white people].
> I'm closer to their image of themselves than I am further away from it ...
> because I can speak English, I can access society in a particular way. But
> it's more than English, it's the way I am, I don't ... appear as threatening.
> I'm familiar.

Through embedding an analysis of distance and proximity to "white people" in her work, Nicole hoped others would see how the language of diversity maintains the exclusion of certain bodies in the City. But Nicole also saw herself being in closer proximity to the somatic norm as a gateway to initiating strategic change in how the City does diversity. In other words, her positioning as a resistant subject became possible through the very diversity terms she sought to challenge. This paradox did not entirely escape Nicole. Being hired for embodying a particular kind of diversity to the exclusion of other racial Others was, as Nicole described it, "the contradiction of our work."

The paradox for racialized staff who seek to destabilize diversity and race in the City is that they are no less embroiled in institutionalized processes of reproducing race and racial exclusion. Although Kevin's and Corey's accounts provide more recognizable examples of resisting prescriptive identities through reproducing race elsewhere, there is a danger in assuming that there are more agentic and critical positionings of ourselves, in diverse institutions and beyond, that are accessed without such paradoxical effects. In fact, assuming such a stance engenders another form of ourselves as being "not like them," reinforcing the very separations which undergird the production of being like no Other in the diverse City.

Regardless of their positionings, racial characteristics were also evoked by staff because they experienced their bodies as raced in the City. Many staff were adamant that, while they may have been seen as "token" diversity hires – hired solely for their race – they proved themselves uniquely worthy of their positions. Tania, for example, explained how she was likely hired to "fill a quota" and was "being used because of my background" but later in our interview explicitly stated that her boss did in fact need someone "friendly, outgoing, and skilled" in his office, so in the end she was a "perfect fit." Moments like this reveal an uncontainable anxiety of *be(com)ing* the unskilled, unqualified racial other Other in the diverse City, hence staff's repetition of the stereotype and assertion of specialized knowledge. If for years the City justified the abjection and exclusion of racial other Others in the diverse City on the grounds of being (their) race, it is entirely possible that staff drew on racial stereotypes and knowledge to distance themselves from race and to demonstrate closer proximity to the somatic norm, for fear of being abjected in the same way. I am thinking here of Michelle's insistence that racial other Others "play that [race] card" or when Stacey explained that certain racialized staff "jump the queue" to get direct access to her when they should be focussed on honing their own competencies and skills. For Stacey, these racialized staff came dangerously close to fulfilling a racial stereotype, teetering on the edge of abjection. These moments also suggest that staff needed to redefine that edge to assure me, others, and perhaps even themselves that they were firmly planted on the right side of abjection's fragile border.

If we take seriously Ahmed's (2004) claim that in the racial encounter emotions like fear gain power and justification through the recirculation of discourses that bind "us" together against Others, then it is equally important for us to think about how diversity discourse in the City of Toronto *produces* the fear of being the abjected racial other Other and then attempts to contain it in the illusion of an in-between third space where staff can do and be diversity differently, in excess of racial thinking, *to regenerate and occlude the production of being like no Other.*[13] The "contradiction," as Nicole referred to it, is that this in-between third space where staff access subjectivities in excess of race might not be as in-between as one might think – or rather, desire.

Native Informing as a Third Space

Many staff also described their specialized knowledge of racialized communities as a way of articulating their capability and trustworthiness in that they could help the white male somatic norm to do diversity better. Staff spoke about how knowing who "the community" is and what the community wants gives them a more authentic view and vantage point of diversity that would always exceed that of their white colleagues. In Sherene's view, sharing this knowledge would help the City to regain its status as "the framework for how diversity works" at local, national and international levels.

But how and under what terms did translating the culture of racial other Others become a tool for racialized staff to justify their positions in the diverse City? How did specialized knowledge of "the community" become a bolstering tactic in negotiations of belonging? Whom does this specialized knowledge serve? As Trinh (1989) reminds us, the native informant is invited into subjectivity through conveying information to outsiders about a native culture only in a way that colonizers can expect and anticipate within their own knowledge systems. The invitation to be the native informant is thus premised on reproducing and further naturalizing the colonial subject as the true bearer of knowledge, power, and the right to claim space. But the fact that staff also see their specialized knowledge as integral to doing diversity better in the City is illuminating in that it presupposes that outsider identities and cultures can still be "known," just *differently*. Again, institutionalized processes that separate knowledgeable insiders Others like no Other from racial other Others to be known are occluded by desires for and articulations of the Self in a third space, where staff access "new" identities in excess of race and in closer proximity to the somatic norm, as knowing subjects. But what the desires of racialized staff to be not-raced, knowing subjects in a third space also powerfully illuminate is that knowing the racial other Other, however flexibly, is a precondition and productive technology of diversity discourse in the City of Toronto, *as it has historically been of race.*

"Not Like Them" Revisited

In bringing together City texts and interview data, I have hopefully begun to explicate how and why the production of racial insider Others like no Other in the diverse City relies on the repetition of racial stereotypes and norms. Interestingly enough, though, City texts contain several moves to explicitly *counter* racial stereotypes. For example, in 1999 the City explicitly condemned a Toronto Police Association's poster that asked voters in the provincial election to "help fight crime by electing candidates who are prepared to take on the drug pushers, the pimps and the rapists" (City of Toronto, 1999d, p. 1) alongside a picture that stereotypically depicts a Hispanic gang. The statement by

City Council condemning the poster, "which promotes racist stereotyping and hostility against the Spanish speaking community," was also touted as one of the many ways in which City Council "demonstrated its political leadership, enhanced its public image, and helped to inspire community attitudes in keeping with the City's commitments in the fields of access, equity, race relations and diversity" (p. 3).

The City of Toronto's (2003a) *Plan of Action for the Elimination of Racism and Discrimination*, led by Diversity Advocate Sherene Shaw, was sparked by the 2000 Ornstein study, which concluded that for ethnoracial minorities with similar education, the levels of unemployment and poverty were significantly higher than for persons of European origin. The City of Toronto Plan identified labour market and economic disparities experienced by racialized communities and offered a series of "diversity strategies,"[14] including "implement programs to assist employees and immigrant workers" (p. 6). Again, the City recommended that mentorship opportunities would alleviate what might otherwise be conceived of as racism. However, immediately following strategies to help those who had not succeeded, the City committed to "publicize and celebrate the success and achievements of diverse people and communities to counter negative stereotypes and help the public understand their contributions to Toronto" (p. 6). In the City's view, countering negative stereotypes would help with "the need for the public to accept and value diversity" (p. 6).

In response to a 2010 *Maclean's* article called "Too Asian?," which advanced the idea that Asian students were limiting the opportunities of non-Asian students in Canadian universities, City Councillor Mike Layton demanded an apology from the magazine for their "negative stereotyping of the Asian-Canadian community." He asked for this apology on behalf of the City of Toronto, which he explained

> has taken a leadership role in working towards building a society in which everyone has the right to live in conditions of dignity, respect and peace ... as a City which respects and values the diversity among our residents which is reflected in the motto, "Diversity Our Strength" ... and has pledged to speak out against incidents of racism and discrimination that can have negative consequences for not only those who are affected but for the community as a whole. (City of Toronto, 2010, p. 1)

In these and other texts countering racial stereotypes, the City makes it clear that it does not tolerate racism and discrimination of any kind. In fact, fighting racism and discrimination is not only woven into the fabric of the diverse City, it is what the City is known for. But as we can see, in countering racial stereotypes the City also recirculates its commitment and leadership in addressing issues of diversity and racism and thus its complete racial innocence. This has specific effects for those who have racial claims, including reproducing the racial stereotypes that underpin their production and justify their abjection. For example, positioning the successes and achievements of racial Others against those who require mentoring in the City of Toronto's (2003a) *Plan of Action for the Elimination of Racism and Discrimination* reinforces the separation between a civilized "us" and uncivilized "them," where the success of racial other Others becomes attainable only through establishing trust and proximity in the City, in a mentoring relationship. In this, racial other Others need not make claims of racism in the diverse City because there is no racism. They simply lack. Those who are not succeeding simply need to learn from those who are established and who belong, in order to succeed and to be *racially palatable*. Disguised as a mutually beneficial opportunity afforded by diversity, in reality, this civilizing principle is, as Goldberg (2009) brilliantly argues, "a mannered racism, even exaggeratedly mannerist, civil to a fault, behaviour by the book" (p. 342).

In addition, although the underlying motive may have been to shift racist ideas, countering negative stereotypes in the Plan of Action was defined and carried out in ways that further naturalized the somatic norm and his power to define the terms under which access and inclusion in his space is granted: as long as "they" are contributing to *my* city in meaningful ways, "they" can be accepted and valued. And, once again, the City conflates racial Other and immigrant. This assumption is deeply raced and also has specific implications for who is seen to naturally and rightfully own, belong and be entitled to space in the City.

Significantly, in explicating what countering racial stereotypes does for the diverse City, we can see how the productive underpinnings of being like no Other are inherently racial *and spatial*. As Hook (2005) reminds us, if we pay explicit attention to processes of subjectification of the stereotype, we can better understand what kinds of identities are momentarily fixed through stereotypical discourses and identifications as well as "what anxieties are alleviated" (p. 9) through this fixity. The question of whether the City reproduces or counters the racial stereotype is thus less important than explicating how and under what terms diversity discourse takes up and is incited by the stereotype, to relieve what kinds of racial anxieties and discursive ruptures, however temporarily.

On Being Like No Other: Final Thoughts

This chapter was intended to work through how the production of racial Others like no Other resonates, is sustained, and has effects up to and including the present moment. In this vein, we might consider how the terms under which the 1993 anti-racism demonstration and its organizers were produced as like no Other inspired, over two decades later, a motion asserting the lack of the capacity for civil behaviour among the Toronto faction of Black Lives Matter. On 6 July 2017, claims of police racism also led Councillors Mammoliti and Karygiannis to ask City Council to offer their full support for Toronto Police in the face of the actions of Black Lives Matter, which, in their words, "vilified," "demonized," "bullied," and "intimidated" Toronto police officers (City of Toronto, 2017a, pp. 1–2). And when Toronto Mayor John Tory employs descriptors like "thugs," "gangsters," and "sewer rats" (NOW Staff, 2018) in reference to recent acts of gun violence in Toronto, we might consider how they reflect deeply institutionalized stereotypes of racial other Others outside of the diverse City – stereotypes that have gained currency and been justified over decades of recirculation and occlusion in the City's diversity discourse.

This chapter also traces the way in which racial lack, civility, and the racial stereotype have historically been incited and come together through diversity discourse to construct and define the parameters of the diverse City as well as who does and does not belong there. These racial tropes are further institutionalized through the production and inclusion of racial Others like no Other, whose bodies come to represent the City's commitments to anti-racism and diversity and in turn legitimize the ongoing abjection of racial other Others on the grounds that they lack. Importantly, racial other Others who make claims of racism in the diverse City are bound to lack not only because they traverse the racial terms that form the what, who, and how of civil interaction, but also because they subvert them. And although we might think that these subversive, uncivilized acts of speaking about racism in "diverse" institutions are dangerous or, as Ahmed (2012) terms, "a breach in the happy image of diversity" (p. 152), I want to stress that racial claims in the diverse City are also productive and formative in terms of racial subjectivity, differential inclusion, and consequently in terms of the City as an innocent space. In the diverse City of Toronto, the inclusion of racial Others like no Other thus wholly depends on the continuity of racism and racial claims.

For racial insider Others, the complexities of navigating, embodying, encountering, performing, and outdoing (their) race in a simultaneously post-racist, post-racial-yet-diverse City are endless and exhausting. Although representations of race in the diverse City might shift, these shifts inevitably become deeply embedded in and indebted to racial discourses and the racializing truths that underpin and are enlivened by them. In this chapter I have explained how the evocation of racial stereotypes and knowledge of racial other Others in interviews with racialized City staff illuminates how staff are produced to further institutionalize and naturalize the somatic norm as knowledgeable and innocent. Gaining trust, proximity, and belonging as racialized staff in the City requires staff to prove that they are "not like them" – racial other Others on the outside who embody historical, representational, and abjection-able traits of race. It also became increasingly clear in interviews that evoking racial stereotypes and specialized knowledge gives racialized staff an escape from being frozen by racial thinking. The rather painful paradox for racialized City staff is that their desires for and articulations of a non-raced Self in a third space of enunciation – a space where Nicole feels "they [the City] can't control my mind, they cannot control my analysis, and they cannot control the way I do my business, right?" – are invited and contained by diversity discourse to reproduce racial other Others in a static, knowable form. The stereotype thus serves a much larger function than one might expect. That the stereotype can facilitate such a sense of freedom and agency for racial insider Others in the diverse City is key to explicating the productive capacity and staying power of race.

In all of this, I hope to have underscored that racialization is relentless. In fact, I have "racialization is relentless" scribbled down in my notes dated 24 March 2015, around the time I first started to think about how, why, and under what terms racial Others are produced to be like no Other in the diverse City. I remember quite vividly why I wrote this. I had just finished rereading transcripts of two interviews, both of which ended in tears. Not only staff's tears, mind you. Years after my stint as political staff at the City, the sense of hopelessness that staff expressed in interviews felt familiar. And still very close.

I originally conceived of this feeling as "diversity fatigue": the work of constantly trying (and failing) to subvert the celebratory rhetoric of diversity to bring in some kind of meaningful action on or at the very least an acknowledgment of racism in the diverse City. In interviews, many described this work as "frustrating," "tiring," and "exasperating," reminding me very much of the interviewees in Ahmed's (2012) book who described diversity work as "banging your head against a brick wall" (p. 26). However, while many staff were "critical" of or resistant to the way diversity was being done in the City, others wholly embraced what diversity stood for. Some described how diversity in the City made them feel "hopeful" and "proud," as staff and as Torontonians. But still, moments of tension crept in. Cracks in the "happy image" of diversity came to the surface.

Yet what all staff had in common, what they all made implicit and sometimes explicit in interviews, was that they did not see themselves as "diverse." I sensed a fatigue here too, but a different kind: one of constantly having to navigate the embodied tensions of potentially *being* "diversity" in the City. Beyond whatever fatigue might arise from what staff "do" with diversity in the City, this was about who they *were*. In this, my conceptualization of diversity fatigue grew. It became important to me to try to understand how staff and other racial Others in the City could all have different and sometimes competing interpretations, ideas, and practices relating to diversity, but all be united in ensuring one thing: being "not like them." What I learned was that racial insider Others in the City did not see themselves as diverse because they were invited and produced to see themselves as being beyond race. I wrote "racialization is relentless" to remind myself that the emotional moments – of tension and/or subversion in interviews and in City texts – were not about navigating diversity in the City. They were about still having to navigate racialization, despite being included like no Other.

I close this chapter by returning to the idea of being the "right kind" of minority in diverse institutions, as those who might deliberately distance themselves from the problem of racism or, as Puwar (2004) explains, those who avoid being "too different and radical" (p. 123) and have the right language, endorsements, and social and cultural capital to remain a trustworthy, "familiar rather than unfamiliar stranger" (p. 128). As I have hopefully made clear, I think of being the right kind of minority in much more complex and pervasive terms. In these last two chapters, the argument I have been trying to build is that racial Others are invited and produced to be exceptional and to be like no Other in the diverse City precisely to be the right kind of minority, in that their subjectivities occlude the reproduction of racial thinking in the diverse City, in the present. As I have shown, critical, resistant, racial insider Others are not immune. As racial insider Others in diverse institutions, it is worth considering that we are all, in some way, the right kind of minority.

I believe it is important to pay close attention to what I think is at the heart of being the right kind of minority in diverse institutions: the desire to be not-raced. As I have argued in this chapter, in the illusion of a third space, the possibilities of and desires for a not-raced identity and the lesser anxieties that might come with it are produced as an effect of the anxieties of diversity discourse and the containment afforded by the space of the diverse City. Diversity discourse produces the very anxieties it then promises to alleviate. As I will argue in the final chapter of this book, explicating how this occurs and under what terms is where I believe agency and resistance can be located.

Chapter Five

Being Through Consultation

On 12 May 2014, Deputy Mayor Norm Kelly and former Chair of the Economic Development Committee City Councillor Michael Thompson convened the first and only Deputy Mayor's Black Business Professionals Roundtable. The objectives of this Roundtable, as noted in the official report of the meeting, were to listen to Black business owners and operators participating, form partnerships, and address the issues Black business owners and operators face by introducing meaningful policies to help them succeed. The report opens with a message from Deputy Mayor Norm Kelly:

> Toronto has a diverse business community that plays an enormous role in the vibrancy of Toronto's economy and social fabric of our communities. At the Deputy Mayor's Black Business Professionals Roundtable, we took an important step towards the formation of a stronger partnership with some of Toronto's Black business owners and operators. The contributions from the participants form the basis for this report and for any initiatives that arise from it. The conversation has only just begun. (City of Toronto, 2014b, p. ii)

After reading this report, I was left with several questions, including why racism wasn't explicitly mentioned anywhere in the report or attached summary notes. Was racism never an issue for "struggling" Black business owners and operators? Perhaps. However, of most concern was how the contributions of the Roundtable participants culminated in a set of recommendations I'd seen several times in City reports offering policy directions on diversity and racism, dating as far back as the 1970s. The recommendations of this report – "building education and awareness," "skills development workshops," and "creating a business professionals mentorship program" for the Black business community – were offered up as ways to help Black businesses "grow and operate efficiently" (p. 9).

How does a meeting that invites Black business owners and operators to discuss the issues they face end up with a set of recommendations that reiterate their lack of training, skills development, and mentoring? By this point in the book, we have all hopefully become more acquainted with the impetus for recommendations like these: the City of Toronto draws on and then imputes familiar historical racial norms onto the bodies of racial Others whose mere presence might hint at the existence of racism, in order to keep the space of the diverse City intact. In this chapter, however, I want us to pay closer attention to how consultation with racial Others in the City of Toronto further enables the City's diversity narrative.

For many scholars, organizations, and policymakers, the City of Toronto's success in achieving diversity (equity, inclusion, and so on) is reflected in the increasing participation of and consultation with racial Others, especially on matters relating to their exclusion (see, e.g., Good, 2009; Graham & Phillips, 2007; Makinde, 2019; Ontario Human Rights Commission, 2010; Qadeer, 2016; Siemiatycki, 2011; Tasan-Kok & Ozogul, 2017). Also explicitly noted in several City of Toronto texts is the City's leadership in prioritizing consultation with racialized groups in their decision-making and policy development. For example, the *International Policy Framework of the City of Toronto* mentions that "the City of Toronto is a leader in developing innovative policies dealing with the issues of ethno-racial diversity and equity," a "trendsetter" because of its principles of "transparency, participation, and inclusive decision-making processes" (City of Toronto, 2002c, p. 9).

While the City's leadership on consulting with racialized groups continues to be circulated both locally and internationally, what is made less clear is *how* racialized groups in Toronto come to be incorporated into decision- and policymaking on diversity and racism in the City, and under what terms. As Ahmed (2012) explains, complaints about race/racism in institutions often get taken up as opportunities to promote organizational values of diversity and to reify the "goodness" of the institution, which can, in effect, contain future complaints. This chapter explores the specific terms under which "complaint" arrives in the City of Toronto. Drawing on interviews with City staff and City texts, I complicate the idea that democracy, political participation, diversity, equity, inclusion, and/or anti-racism are achieved via consultation with racial Others in the City. In this, I challenge the idea that engaging *more* racial Others is key to challenging racism in the City.[1] I conclude by continuing my discussion on the relationship(s) between subjectivity, belonging, and desire. Specifically, I contend that the belonging and desires of racial insider Others to be not-raced again depend on and are incited by the reproduction of racialization and race.

Consultation, Democracy, and Diversity

Many racialized City staff I interviewed promoted consultation as a way for the City to achieve its goals of becoming a truly "diverse" City, even as they acknowledged flaws in the consultation process. For example, Lauren described how consultation ensures that Toronto residents have "the opportunity to participate as much as possible in the decision-making process," but was quite critical of how the City interprets, promotes, and encourages diversity in consultation "on a very narrow level": a "ticking of boxes.... [A]t a public meeting you must be accessible, and must offer translation services and be wheelchair accessible, and so on." For Lauren, a deeper and more critical engagement with diversity in consultation processes would "bring a broader range of views and opinions and perspectives and backgrounds to the City," but with the overarching goal of changing the way decisions in the City are made, and by whom.

Many staff echoed Lauren's concerns about the City's superficial engagement with diversity in consultations. They argued that the City lacked meaningful participation, consultation, and engagement with racialized and other excluded communities. Corey, for example, described how "people with more time to come out, more privileged people" are often the ones who show up at community consultations. In fact, this is how he thinks the City came to choose the motto "Diversity Our Strength," after consulting with "particular groups of privileged people with an agenda, who are interested in presenting Toronto to the world in a particular way." Corey was also critical of the ways in which "marginalized communities are sometimes invited to contribute their thoughts on particular issues, but then the decisions made are left to the politicians." Staff thus saw increasing meaningful participation as an integral part of their work.

For some, bringing in the perspectives of racialized and other marginalized communities would not only change the City's diversity policies and practices, it would directly challenge traditional, hegemonic whiteness in the institution. As Michelle said of consultations in the City, "Only the white people come out." Nicole elaborated on this point:

How can we build a democratic structure of community input, which is over and beyond town halls, because town halls and official consultations

... only the usual suspects show up. So this is the conversation. How can we have a permanent mechanism or series of mechanisms, and how can we recruit? And how can we actually have access or create access for those communities that don't have a sense of entitlement? They don't get to have their voice heard. *How can we get to them?*

While several racialized staff saw consultation processes as a means to challenge diversity policies and practices in the City, in the rest of this chapter I introduce a series of critical interventions to posit that the desires to incorporate more racialized and other marginalized voices in the City are an effect and *affect* of diversity discourse in the City. In this, a sort of "consultation paradox" emerges: the invitation to racial Others to speak about race/racism in the diverse City reproduces racialization and race at the very moment that it purports to undo them.

This paradox crystallized as I reflected on my interview with Sherene. While Sherene believed that "doing diversity properly" in the City can mean "consulting with your population, with your people," she explained how consultations in the City were particularly effective with Aboriginal populations because they are kept "purposefully separate from the diversity you're talking about." These "purposefully separate" consultations led to the establishment of the City's Aboriginal Affairs Advisory Committee, comprising 13 Aboriginal members who "use their knowledge and expertise to initiate key Aboriginal-focused policies, such as the Statement of Commitment to the Aboriginal communities and the Aboriginal Employment Strategy." For Sherene, the establishment of this Committee contributes significantly to the City's leadership in the areas of access and equity, locally and globally, because it shows the City's commitment to consulting with Aboriginal communities in decision-making and to "increasing the Aboriginal representation in our workforce" in particular.

Yet when I asked if she thought the Committee's work to increase representation over the past few years will actually change hiring practices in the City, Sherene replied,

> Ah, gosh [*laughs*]. No [*laughs*]. A lot has to happen in terms of hiring and that would be if the City of Toronto said, well ... we're only going to hire, target this to the Aboriginal community. But that won't ever happen, I don't think. I can't see that happening.

I use this interview as a starting point into a critical interrogation of how consultations with racial Others can reconstitute racialization and race in the City. Sherene described consultation as one of the only ways to keep Aboriginal communities from being caught up in what she called "the typical diversity policies and actions" of the City. However, as I later discovered in my review of City "consultation" texts, the recommendations of the City's Aboriginal Affairs Advisory Committee often followed exactly those contained in the City's "diversity" policies. These recommendations included representation, training, mentoring, and skills development for Aboriginal communities and/or "cultural competency training for existing staff" to better understand the Aboriginal community.[2] Sherene also alluded to consulting with Others and the commitments that arise from them as merely *symbolic* gestures; yet she and others I interviewed continued to stand behind them as mechanisms for change. The question I was left with was: what does consultation with racial Others *do* for racialized City staff?

I am reminded here of some of the statements I heard in interviews: "If we wrote about racism [in City reports], no one would read them." "If I talked about racism in the City, I'd, I'd probably get blown out the window." Indeed, for many staff, bringing other racial Others in to challenge diversity discourse, race, and racism in the City can also mean depending on these racial "outsiders" to make race-based claims that staff are bound by diversity discourse and the terms of belonging in the City to not make themselves. But herein lies this rather elusive "consultation paradox": while consultation with racial Others might encourage race-based claims in the City, consultation also reproduces the encounter with racial Others and the terms of their abjection that are necessary to *the very discourse that many staff seek to challenge*. An additional paradox emerges when we consider that Sherene and other racialized staff who invite and promote more consultation with racial Others to challenge diversity discourse, race, and racism in the City are doing exactly what they have been produced to do.

As Ahmed (2002) reminds us, "It is in such face-to-face encounters that bodies become racialized" (p. 56). I turn now to City of Toronto texts that advocate for/seek out consultation with racial Others so that the City can become better at "doing" diversity, democracy, and/or addressing issues of race. Illuminating what these texts do with race and/or racial claims in the City and within what larger, textually mediated processes is, I argue, crucial to understanding how the familiar historical racial norms of diversity discourse are simultaneously reproduced *and occluded* through consultation.

Being Through Commodification

What I resent most, however, is not his inheritance of a power he so often dis-
claims, disengaging himself from a system he carries with him, but his ear, eye,
and pen, which record in his language while pretending to speak through mine,
on my behalf.

Trinh T. Minh-ha (1989, p. 48)

That to speak is to exist absolutely for the other.

Franz Fanon (1952, p. 1)

bell hooks (1992) describes how the presence of the racial Other in institutional spaces can be offered up as a sign that progressive change is happening, as long as the Other is consumed and commodified in a recognizable form, to reconfirm whiteness and power. This commodified, recognizable form often relies on stereotypes of the "primitive" racial Other that
are rooted in the idea of "traditional" cultures and lifestyles. Importantly,
this commodified form of racial otherness is desired only in quantities that
do not undermine or threaten white dominance in any way – a "spice,
seasoning, that can liven up the dull dish that is mainstream white culture" (p. 21). Through commodification, voices of non-white Others are
first enabled and then "eaten, consumed, and forgotten" (p. 26).

Thus far, I have explored how diversity discourse in the City of Toronto
both evokes and reproduces racial norms to essentialize racial Others,
thereby reframing and/or refusing racial claims. Some of the texts I have
drawn on have evolved from consultations with racial Others in the City.
However, following hooks, I focus now on how consultation serves specifically to invite and then commodify racial Others as Other, to signal
proof of the City's accountability and progress on race, and to maintain
the space of the City as an exceptionally diverse and innocent space.

For example, the *Framework for Citizen Participation in the City of
Toronto* proposes a forum with Toronto citizens along with "elected
officials, researchers and members of academia from other cities" (City
of Toronto, 1999b, p. 4) to discuss best practices for civic engagement.
In this text, the City explicitly notes its commitment "to include the
diversity of community groups in public consultation processes" and
outlines its ongoing efforts to remove barriers to access and to "increase
the presence of marginalized groups" in the political decision-making
process. These efforts include how "information pamphlets and bro-
chures are usually translated into different languages in order to facilitate their accessibility to different language groups" (p. 3).

In interviews several staff referred to these "translation" tropes as the problematic pinnacle of the City's diversity work. Here, we should pay close attention to how translation emerges and is recirculated as part of the City's commitment to consult with more "marginalized" (read: racialized) groups. Consultation with racial Others thus becomes both the trigger and mechanism through which to recirculate the historical racial norms of diversity discourse – in this case, an essential lack of language skills in racial Others – to not only occlude racism in the City, but also to enable the City's narrative of being committed to diversity *for addressing this lack* (via translation). The irony is that the terms under which consultation with racial Others is authorized and carried out in the diverse City actually enable and justify their ongoing exclusion.

Importantly, there are cases where racism is explicitly named as the *cause* for consultation with racial Others. To prepare for the City of Toronto's (2003a) *Plan of Action for the Elimination of Racism and Discrimination*, approximately 50 community consultation sessions were held, bringing in over 1,000 people to contribute their thoughts on how the City could combat increasing experiences of racism and discrimination in Toronto. In the summary notes of the consultations were several statements about experiences of racism in Toronto:

> Since 9/11, Muslim is a euphemism for walking bomb.
> Racism is a growing problem in Toronto. How do I know? I know because the number of attacks on me keeps increasing.
> There is no safe place. (p. 29)

The City's accountability (or lack thereof) in addressing racism was also explicitly noted in the summary:

> Participants expressed frustration that they were being consulted again. Individuals and community groups asked why they were being consulted when the City and other governments had a catalogue of actions that could be taken. (p. 27)

Yet in the body of the Plan, these and other comments made by "consulted" racial Others are commodified and reframed to perpetuate the City's diversity narrative:

> Diversity is a fundamental characteristic of our city. It gives Toronto strength through an ability to value, celebrate and respect differences. It is this recognition of diversity, which makes *Toronto one of the most creative, caring and successful cities in the world*. (p. 20; my emphasis)

The Council Reference Group invited residents, community groups and organizations to offer help and input to build the Plan of Action for the Elimination of Racism and Discrimination. The Reference Group proposed that the Plan of Action *build on the legacy and leadership for which the City is known.* (p. 25; my emphasis)

They welcomed the opportunity to participate in these consultations with one of the few orders of government where discussion on issues of diversity is taking place. Participants expressed hope that the City of Toronto would continue to act as an advocate on behalf of its residents despite the current political climate, and that the *City would continue to lead the country in addressing issues of diversity.* (p. 28; my emphasis)

As Cheng (2001) reminds us, institutional spaces "often do not want to fully expel the racial other; instead, they wish to maintain that other within existing structures.... [T]hey need the very thing they hate or fear" (p. 12). I want to extend Cheng's analyses to state perhaps the most crucial point of this chapter: "consulted" racial Others and their racial claims are necessary to and *constitutive of* the City's diversity narrative. If we begin with this, we can then consider how even the mere presence of "consulted" racial Others in the City is always-already commodified to *confirm* the City's commitment to diversity and progress on race, regardless of what participants might contribute and, perhaps more importantly, regardless of what policies and practices are put in place to address racism. The question of outcomes, including how many policies and practices to address racism have actually been carried out, also becomes absorbed into the continuous, discursive reframing of presence. This, I argue, is also the basis of Good's (2009) claim that community organization leaders representing immigrant and ethnocultural minorities would not continue to take an active role in the City's consultations on diversity and racism if the City had not already been highly responsive to their needs.

As we can also see in the Plan of Action, racial claims – what Ahmed terms "complaints" – are depoliticized and commodified, to signal "proof" of progress and institutional accountability on issues of race. They are, as Ahmed (2019) brilliantly posits, "stopped from getting through or getting out as the sound of institutions at work" (para 7). There is, after all, a certain irony in stating that diversity makes Toronto one of the most caring cities in the world, in a report that explicitly seeks to address heightened experiences of racism and discrimination in its midst. Those who experience racism and increasing racial attacks, and who feel unsafe because of their race and/or religion would hardly call Toronto "caring." But we would be remiss to think that complaints are completely contained by institutionalized diversity tactics in the City of Toronto, or even that they are wholly deemed as the "problem," particularly when we begin to understand complaints as being necessary prerequisites and *effects* of the diverse City narrative. In this, racial complaints can even be *solicited* by the City of Toronto to ensure the continuity of the City's diversity narrative, and it is precisely because these complaints are never fully addressed by diversity that they return when solicited again, only to be commodified again. And the cycle continues.

Returning to Rose's (1996) contention that the space of war invents new, inevitably containable subjectivities that keep discourse and power intact, I am suggesting we pay close attention to how consultation facilitates the inclusion of racial complaints through which to invent new subjectivities that simultaneously produce and contain "new" challenges to diversity. Put differently, *consultation with racial Others is, quite literally, diversity's space of war*. It is where both global and local racial violences are translated, at the local level, into demands for government accountability and action, and also where the binds of diversity discourse are most tested; where its limitations and anxieties are provoked. These claims have certainly contributed to spurring shifts in institutionalized discourses and with them, a host of policy interventions and even direct action. Of course, tracing the actual implementation of policy recommendations that arise out of consultation(s) is a different project – one that might also trace the nuances of the relationship between participation and action in light of other "persuasive" local and global contexts.

Nevertheless, there is a delicate balance here. Consultation in itself can signify and be touted as anti-racist action, particularly in diverse yet institutionally white spaces. As Paschel (2016) writes, consultation spaces designed to meet new and/or increasing racial claims can also provide the state with a way to "institutionalize dissent" (p. 200).[3] I have shown some of the ways this is done in the City of Toronto: claims about racism and/or the inadequacies of diversity rhetoric in addressing racism in the City have incited new ways (and opportunities) to suture the limitations and anxieties of diversity via reproducing the racial norms and erasures that make it up. What this also means, as I have discussed elsewhere (Almeida 2016, 2018, 2019; Joseph et al., 2019), is that "resistant" racial subjects can have a role in keeping the racial norms of diversity going.

Consulting the Same

Some City texts also recommend additional consultations with select "consulted" racial Others. For example, in 1991 the Toronto Mayor's Committee on Community and Race Relations held a public meeting, given the poor relations between the Black community and Toronto Police, "to hear from all spectrums of the Black Community about those relations and to avail the Black Community of an opportunity to express those concerns and give the Committee input on changes to the Police Act" (City of Toronto, 1991a, p. 204). The meeting resulted in a recommendation of further "private meetings between the Mayor, some members of the Committee, and the Black Community, to restore mutual respect and trust between the Black Community and the police" (p. 204).

The 29 October 2002 *Notice of Motion: Principle of Zero Tolerance of Racial Profiling for Policing in the City of Toronto* put forward by Councillor Shaw and seconded by Councillor Balkissoon outlines the unjust and purposeful targeting of "members of the Black community" (City of Toronto, 2002d, p. 1) by Toronto Police, including racial profiling, police traffic stops and searches, and other forms of discriminatory treatment. The motion also references several reports over three decades on racial profiling of the Black community in Toronto, many with outstanding recommendations. Recommendations include "hiring the required number of Police officers to reflect the ethnic compilation of the City of Toronto," "diversity training programs to ensure police officers have the appropriate skills and training for policing within our diverse communities," and that a "Toronto Police Services Board Race Relations Policy Advisory Committee" be established, comprising members of the Toronto Police Services Board, members of Toronto City Council, and "members of diverse communities" (p. 2).

In response to the Motion, Police Chief Julian Fantino "met with members of the Black community" and subsequently made commitments to "enhance the TPS recruit orientation and training programs by arranging face to face meetings with police recruits and members of the Black community prior to their graduation" and "to coordinate a Race Relations Conference in Toronto where the TPS, the Black community and all levels of civil society/government focus on problem solving" (City of Toronto, 2003b, p. 7). Attached to this report is the City of Toronto's Race and Ethnic Relations Committee submission that "sufficient studies and reports have been prepared on the subject of racial profiling and systemic racism over the last 27 years" and "now time for action on this important matter" (p. 21). The action the Committee recommends is that the African Legal Clinic, the Toronto Police Services Board, and other stakeholders – those already consulted numerous times on racial profiling in Toronto – be invited to make deputations to the 23 January 2003 meeting of City Council.

The meeting of the Black Business Professionals Roundtable meeting I discussed at the beginning of this chapter also recommends the constitution of a "Black Business Professionals Program Advisory Committee" (City of Toronto, 2014b, p. 4) comprising key stakeholders and members from the Roundtable meeting, to provide ongoing advice to the City on the lack of success among Black business owners and operators in Toronto.

As I discovered in my research, repeat consultations are most often recommended in response to what the City has in more recent years officially called anti-Black racism. Historically, these repeat consultations have often invited the same "consulted" individuals and groups from Toronto's Black communities to continue discussions on policing, racial profiling, support for Black-owned businesses, and the lack of representation of Black employees in the Toronto Public Service.[4]

Following my arguments in the previous chapter, being invited back into consultation can also certainly be premised on achieving a certain level of civility, trust with, and proximity to the somatic norm. But the idea that only those who perform "right kind of minority" scripts are invited to return is again, dangerously simplistic. Instead, I suggest that the invitation to return is in itself a productive, *civilizing institutional practice of diversity*. In this approach, surmising which racial Others are invited back and under what terms becomes less important than tracing the discursive permissions afforded by repeat consultations that increasingly seek to produce and envelop those at the "margins" of diversity, *including those who do not participate*. As Ahmed (2012) writes, those who speak about racism in "diverse" institutions are constructed as angry figures who are simply unwilling to put histories of racism behind them. I contend that in the City of Toronto and under the racial norms of diversity discourse, repeat consultations with Black Torontonians in particular additionally produce and emphasize the "angry" Black outsider figure who lacks the ability and civility to "put racism behind them" and thus refuses to participate on defensive grounds.

Take, for example the media reports that emphasized the *absence* of Black Lives Matter Toronto during the City's numerous consultations in preparation for the City's *Toronto Action Plan to Confront Anti-Black Racism*.[5] One such report, from CBC News (2016, 18 April), begins with Toronto Mayor John Tory's offer to meet with Black Lives Matter Toronto to discuss policing issues – an offer that, in Mayor Tory's own words, "has been not just not responded to, it's been absolutely rejected. And that's fine, but I'm just saying that I want to move forward."

Importantly, Mayor Tory positions the absence and generally angry, "uncooperative" spirit of Black Lives Matter Toronto against the *other community leaders who are people that I think can give me some advice on how we really address the core issue here*" (my emphasis).

In this report, as in others, we can see how *not* participating in the City's consultations can be an equally powerful tool of the City's diversity narrative. Not participating not only reaffirms the historical, racial norms of diversity discourse that associates racial outsiders with incivility and lacking the ability to "move forward," as Tory himself suggests; racial outsiders are also then held almost exclusively responsible for both their own racial "demise" and any lack of progress in the City on issues of race. Repeat consultations in the diverse City thus stand in for and *as* action on issues of race – anti-Black racism in particular – while also producing "new" discursive boundaries and subjectivities through which any semblance of inaction on the City's part can be contained.

Fanon (1952) writes, "There is a quest for the black man. He is yearned for, white men can't get along without him. He is in demand, but they want him seasoned a certain way" (p. 152). Ahmed (2012) draws on Fanon's work to also remind us that bodies become racialized through the encounter. Historically, white and Black bodies were produced as ontologically and epistemologically different, such as through civil/uncivil and moral/immoral dichotomies, both as a function and justification of the colonial project. And yet the "seasoning" doled out by Mayor Tory transfers these historical racial tropes to separate Black bodies *from each other*. This, I argue, is an effect and affect of discursive and material racial inclusion, necessary to the City's diversity narrative, but also anxiety-producing. Importantly, the anxieties of inclusion in the diverse City can also include *refusal* of the encounter, and by extension, the racial tropes (and democratic claims) that are reproduced through it. Refusal also triggers psychic anxieties; it is, after all, through meeting the Other that the subject "is determined to keep his own superiority" (Fanon, 1952, p. 186).

In the diverse City, these anxieties are recovered through again attending to physical and racial proximity, separating Others who are just close enough from Others who are too close. The space of the diverse City and the claims that bind it further entrench Black "outsiders" as also fundamentally *anti-democratic*, in liberal terms. We can also learn here that the commodification and subjectivization of Black bodies under the racial norms of diversity discourse do not necessitate their actual inclusion and/or presence in the diverse City, as hooks (1992) might suggest.

Commodification Through Recirculation

Perhaps most surprising in my research was the degree to which "consulted" racial Others are further commodified through recirculation in City texts. For example, at the March 1998 meeting of Toronto City Council, a Task Force on Community Access and Equity was created to ensure that diverse, equity-seeking communities in Toronto continued to have a voice in decision- and policymaking in the City, post-amalgamation. Comprising City Councillors and City staff, the Task Force was charged to "strengthen community involvement and public participation in the decision-making processes of the municipality, particularly for equity seeking communities" and "ensure that the contributions, interests and needs of all sectors of Toronto's diverse population are reflected in the City's mission, operation and service delivery" (City of Toronto, 1998b, p. 1). In the terms of reference for the Task Force, these equity-seeking communities – "women, people of colour, Aboriginal people, people with disabilities, lesbians and gays, immigrants/refugees, different religious/faith communities" – are used interchangeably with "Toronto's diverse population" (p. 1). The Task Force held several City-wide consultation meetings, where they reported hearing community members' concerns, including increases in hate crimes, difficulties in gaining Canadian work experience, and barriers to accessing City services.

In the final report, Chair of the Task Force City Councillor Joe Mihevc listed the Task Force's most significant accomplishment: the establishment of Community Advisory Committees and working groups, made up of two-thirds community "experts" who were to give advice to City Council on "issues of access, equity and human rights" (City of Toronto, 1999a, p. 2). In the report, Councillor Mihevc also summarizes the Committees' and working groups' feelings about their contributions in the City:

> Members of the groups have very positive feelings about the past and ongoing efforts of the City to be an advocate to other levels of government and to respond to the diverse service needs of its population. *Community members also stressed that the assembly of people from all corners of the world living and working in the City has created a social fabric that is the envy of many.* (p. 3; my emphasis)

Although the Committees and working groups represented marginalized communities, their establishment travels across several texts over several years to demonstrate the City's leadership *in addressing racism in particular*:

> Toronto City Council has undertaken the following as part of its commitment to the elimination of racism and discrimination in this City: Established Community Advisory Committees on Access, Equity and Human Rights. (City of Toronto, 2001a, p. 7)
>
> The City of Toronto is a leader in developing innovative policies dealing with the issues of ethnoracial diversity and equity. For instance, the City of Toronto adopted the Report of the Task Force on Community Access and Equity.... The City of Toronto can share valuable expertise and knowledge with cities around the globe about these management practices. (City of Toronto, 2002a, p. 12)
>
> Active involvement by Toronto's diverse communities is in line with the trend for enhanced local democracy and public accountability and opening up the process of local government ... as demonstrated by the specific advisory bodies established by Council to address access, equity and human rights issues. (City of Toronto, 2006, p. 3)

Importantly, the Task Force, Committees, and working groups are also circulated by scholars and organizations *several years after their inception*, as proof that the City of Toronto is proactive in addressing diversity, democracy, and racism. As Ahmed (2012) argues, the recirculation of diversity in texts stands in for (in)action on addressing racism. However, I also offer that in the City of Toronto, it is the circulation of consultation with racial Others in texts across time that furthers the commodification of racial Others and regenerates the confluence of diversity discourse and the historical, familiar norms of race.

Yet perhaps most powerful about the practice of recirculation is how it intensifies affect (Ahmed, 2004). Building upon my argument on affect in Chapter 4, I suggest that the more diversity discourse and consultation recirculate, the more they contain and reproduce signs of achieving the ideals of diversity, racial inclusion, and democracy. As such, it is my contention that the recirculation of diversity discourse and consultation, in tandem, acts as an *affective technology*. Recirculation can certainly elicit pride in being diverse, post-racist, democratic, and so on, which binds the diverse City against other "less progressive" spaces and, perhaps more importantly, assuages both the need for and anxieties about close(r) encounters with "difference," as Ahmed (2004) and Hook (2005) suggest. But we mustn't forget that racialized City staff also encourage, recirculate, and re-cite more consultations with racial Others as a way to *transform* diversity policies and practices. The impetus of racialized City staff to include more racial Others in decision-making in the City might certainly be to address and challenge racial barriers to participation, and as a way to negotiate and imagine new forms of belonging for racial Others in the City. What we must also consider is that promoting consultation with more racial Others also bolsters the belonging of racialized staff, *as insiders who have the capacity to bring outsiders in.* Indeed, some staff even articulated this capacity as exceptionally theirs. In this, recirculation further aligns the ideals, instrumentations, and "self-regulative practices" (Hook, 2007, p. 216) of the racial Self/subject as not-raced – contained via specific forms of racial inclusion in the diverse City – with the broader political objectives and practices of government.

This exceptional capacity is an important marker of the intersections of diversity discourse, consultation, subjectivity, and belonging. "Bringing outsiders in," as we learned from my conversation with Sherene, has come to exemplify change/resistance/war in itself, thereby occluding what actually happens when outsider voices *are* included and under what terms. But the capacity of staff to incorporate more racialized voices is also an integral part of how staff articulate their Selves. Again, and in relation to diversity discourse and consultation, this is not about what staff *do*; rather, it is about who they *are*. In this case, racialized City staff as "insider Others" become bound and contained to aligning their identities and ideals with the performative practices of diversity discourse in the diverse City; importantly, both *require the race-claims of other Others/outsiders.*

Through Consultation: Final Thoughts

Critiquing the idea of radical democracy in the West, Dhaliwal (1996) argues that exclusions constitute the formation of liberal democracies. Democracy and inclusion discourses often miss (or, I would argue, occlude) how racial Others can be selectively included to reproduce a hegemonic Self, to "reaffirm a hegemonic core to which the margins are added without any significant destabilization of the core or continue to valorize the very centre that is problematic to begin with" (p. 44). For Dhaliwal, the motivation to increase democratic participation and inclusion of marginalized/racialized Others thus needs to be questioned, in the context of reproducing Western superiority and colonial relationships.

This chapter has taken up Dhaliwal's desire to question the motivation for democratic inclusion politics as well as Butler's (2011) theorization of the constitutive outside to suggest that the democratic participation of racial Others in the diverse City is premised on the commodification of bodies who make racial claims. I have drawn on several City "consultation" texts to show how the presence and claims of racial Others, institutionalized through Committees, Advisory Bodies, and other means of consultation, are reframed as "proof" of the City's leadership in enhancing democratic participation and engaging racialized communities in decision-making, regardless of what their contributions might actually be. I have also offered that it is through hailing the desires to be not-raced that the racializing terms under which consultations are held and repeated become occluded, in speech acts and through text. As I discovered in my research on consultation, the sense of the City of Toronto as a leader on diversity and racism is maintained and reproduced in large part because of racism. Put differently, the City *requires racism*, in order to continue its claims of being increasingly democratic and progressive. The City also reproduces race, at the very moment that it claims its undoing via consultation with racialized groups. This is the violence of diversity discourse in the City: racial Others and their experiences of racism exist solely as vessels for its reproduction(s).

Race as Pleasure

Whiteness is not a color; it is a way of feeling pleasure in and about one's body.
                                                            Anthony Farley (1997, p. 457)

Farley's (1997) intervention on race as a form of pleasure is also an important facet to consider when thinking through consultation with racial Others on racism in relation to commodification and/or the reproduction of race. As he argues, white subjects experience pleasure in the body when they humiliate the Black body and then deny that race/racism exists in the first place. The *denial* is the greatest injury to the Black body, more painful than the original humiliation. The pleasure of race is also derived from the white subject's continual gaze on the Black body's inferiority and subordination, confirming over and over again for white subjects that they indeed are on the right side of the colour line while also satisfying "a self-created urge to be white" (p. 463).[6] It is in these moments of denial and desire that Black pain is translated into white power.

Farley argues that the state is especially instrumental in creating spaces for race-pleasure to occur, through the repeated itemization, narration, structuring, and denial of the colourline. He describes the mechanisms through which it is done:

> [R]ace-pleasure may be obtained directly or textually. The direct pleasure in saying "Look, a Negro!" is akin to the textual pleasure of talking, read-

ing, writing, or thinking about the "black problem." The discourse of race involves lavishly decorating the black body with statistics, stories, and images of violence, narcotics, illiteracy, illegitimacy, and disease. (p. 475)

In the City of Toronto, consultations with racial Others on issues of racism provide the conditions of possibility for the race-pleasure that Farley describes. As I have shown, it is also where racial Others have been recast as bodies to be consumed, pacified, and/or erased, directly and textually. But I am also reminded here of the consultations on issues of racism I attended when I was a placement student and then as political staff in the City: watching racialized Toronto residents share their painful experiences with an audience made up of politicians, staff, organization representatives, advocacy and community groups, and/or other residents. I remember the feeling in the room as the more detailed or painful experiences were being shared. There were audible gasps, sometimes also tears. I remember watching as people – mostly white staff and other white bystanders – put their hands to their chests, breathing deeply. The pain being shared was absolutely palpable. But as people left the meeting, there were collective sighs of relief. I heard people exclaim things like, "Whew! That was rough!" or "I never knew how bad it was." I remember feeling quite uneasy, hearing this. It was only recently that I began to think that these might have been expressions of race-pleasure. Not knowing how bad it is can also be a form of pleasure-via-denial.

One aim of this book is to get us thinking more critically about the idea that the inclusion of racial Others in diverse institutions necessitates progressive, anti-racist change. Race-pleasure helps us to understand how one form of racial inclusion, the "democratic participation" of racial Others in the state, can be violent. In these last three chapters, I hope I have also underscored that when we think of achieving progress and institutional change solely in terms of racial inclusion, we miss how racial subjectivities can be produced, enabled, and contained to reproduce historical, racial norms that uphold whiteness in institutions.

I also argue that diversity discourse in the City of Toronto does not determine who is "outside." It *makes* outsiders. Consultation with racial Others is an integral part of making outsiders. The question that remains is whether, if diversity makes outsiders in order to reconstitute itself, must racial "insider Others" do the same to reconstitute their belonging. I hope that I have begun to illuminate in these last three chapters that if diversity discourse in the City of Toronto reconstitutes itself via abjection of racial other Others/outsiders, the subject positionings that

animate and are contained by diversity discourse in the City of Toronto –
those who are "inside" – *must do the same and are produced to do the same.*
As I have shown, "insider" positionings that constitute and are constituted by diversity discourse (and the racial norms that are incited into
it) are made intelligible in the City via their varied remaking and refusal
of racial outsiders.

In her colonial reading of Foucault's work on European sexuality,
Stoler (1995) writes that desire follows from and is generated out of discourses of sexuality "where it is both animated and addressed" (p. 165).
As such, critical interrogations into the relationships between discourse
and desire must not begin with the "true" knowledge of desire itself, but
with how desire is both constituted and constituting. Following Stoler,
I suggest that the desires to be not-raced emerge from and reproduce
the racializing and racially normative conditions of diversity discourse.
This means that, yes, diversity discourse reproduces race, but also that
the desires to be not-raced are invited, regulated, and released *through
that reproduction.* Racial subjects of diversity discourse in the City of
Toronto thus experience desire as an effect and *affect* of diversity.

In this vein, I suggest again that we move away from the idea that
attaining greater participation and inclusion means we have "solved"
the problem of racism in the City of Toronto and beyond. Instead, I
ask that we investigate, illuminate, share, and then begin to disrupt the
racial practices that are legitimized through diversity and other discourses to reinscribe race and power. As I stated in the outset of this
book, when we trace and share how diversity discourse and race manifest and under what terms, we can begin to build a global reservoir of
knowledge and strategies that seek to undermine their re-authorizations,
in and across institutions.

In 2017, the City of Toronto initiated 41 "community conversations"
across Toronto in preparation for the *Toronto Action Plan to Confront
Anti-Black Racism* (City of Toronto, 2017e). Over 800 self-identified
Black Torontonians participated. In preparation for the consultations,
an extensive review of reports on racism submitted to the City over
the past 41 years by "Black leaders, activists, educators, community
groups and public servants" (p. 5) was conducted to determine if the
City had acted upon their recommendations. The review showed that
few actions had been taken.

Although the Action Plan states that the review was conducted by
the City of Toronto and "Black leaders and organizations" (p. 5), it does
not disclose from where (or whom) the idea for the review originated.
However, unique to this Plan's process and overall strategy is that consultation with racial Others became the mechanism by which to hold the

City accountable for both its inaction and commodification, which then justified a series of institutionalized measures centred solely on tracking implementation of the new Plan's recommendations and actions.

Whether this strategy will work, only time will tell. As I write this, the recommendations of the Anti-Black Racism Plan are slowly being carried out. Governments in Canada, Germany, Sweden, Australia, the United Kingdom, New Zealand, Ireland, Brazil, South Africa, the United States, and elsewhere are responding to the current global, political climate demanding justice for Black, Indigenous, and people of colour (BIPOC) communities experiencing violence at the hands of the state by engaging these groups in decision- and policymaking, under the auspices of achieving truly integrated, diverse, inclusive, democratic, anti-racist and/or decolonized societies. While some have, in their respective locations, also argued that consultations generally co-opt the presence of racialized and Indigenous groups (see, e.g., Abu-Laban & Gabriel, 2002; Back et al., 2009; Bhavnani et al., 2005; Came, 2014; Cowen & Parlette, 2011; Fakier, 2018; Green, 2017; Mascarenhas, 2012), Paschel (2016) showed us in intricate detail how the participation of Black social movement actors in state consultations led to the official recognition of Black rights in Brazil. The more nuanced details – such as which "consulted" group contributions actually shape government policies aimed at combating racism and how, which contributions are considered "illegitimate" and under what terms, and the larger historical, political, and racial landscapes, forces and tensions that produce and/or hinder government consultations, policies, and actions to address racism – are severely lacking. This is an important knowledge gap that I hope to tackle in future work.

The next and final chapter of this book continues my examination and discussion of the possibilities of agency in the diverse City. Building on Davies's (2000) conceptualization of agency as an awareness of the containment of desire(s) in discourse, I discuss how contradictions and erasures, once made visible, become a site of agency via an interruption of the idea of our Selves and our desires as continuous, essential, individualized, and autonomous. I ask, in emphasizing a move away from the "rational, autonomous Self" (and the binaries/dualisms thus implied), is it possible to embrace these contradictions as part of an understanding of how subjectivity is experienced and not authored by our Selves? What happens to discursive constitutions and subjectivities when they are spoken and written in terms of contradictions, complicities, abjections, and erasures?

Chapter Six

On Diversity Discourse and the Problem of Agency

[T]he individual assumes that she is the author of the ideology or discourse which she is speaking. She speaks or thinks as if she were in control of meaning. She imagines that she is indeed the type of subject which humanism proposes – rational, unified, the source rather than the effect of language.

Chris Weedon (1997, p. 31)

So what now? No matter where I go, whether I am discussing this research at local and international conferences, events, or at gatherings with colleagues, I am asked this question. I was warned that if I chose to pursue a project that sought to trace how we are never operating "outside the bounds of power" (Hook, 2007, p. 70), the implication was that I was choosing a "determinist" stance, one that identifies the historicity and productive effects of power but offers very little possibility of the subject as an agent of change. The discussion I pursue in this final chapter, on the possibilities of agency under diversity discourse in the City of Toronto, might seem deterministic at first. I argue in this chapter that agency for racial Others in the City of Toronto under the racial norms of diversity discourse cannot exist "outside the bounds of power" (Carrillo Rowe, 2005, p. 21). This position can be and is often seen as somewhat pessimistic, especially when racial subjects are interpreted to be no more than passive conduits of power/knowledge (Caldwell, 2007). My other writings tracing how we as racial Others can participate in power, whiteness, racial thinking, and so on have led to some tense conversations with my racialized colleagues, centred upon the idea that I appear to be blaming racial Others when all we are trying to do is foster change in our "diverse" institutional spaces.

But blame is not, nor has it ever been, my goal. In my view, the key to agency and to any type of sociopolitical change in our respective spaces and beyond is to first determine how and under what terms we participate in power and prop it up. In this, discomfort with ourselves as "agents of change" and hopefully what that discomfort leads to *is a good thing*. In this vein, I ask that we consider this project of exposing the racial(izing) norms of diversity discourse and the subject positions that reproduce and are reproduced by them as a site of illumination into the modes of complicity with power as well as the contradictions that are transformed and/or muted through our (re-)making of racial Others into diverse subjects in the City of Toronto. As I have written elsewhere (Almeida, 2019), we might also take these analyses of the confluence of diversity discourse, race, subjectivity, and belonging in a local site such as the City of Toronto as an opportunity to consider complicity across the globe – especially if we seek to undo race, racism, and their effects.

Before I turn to the matter of agency and diversity discourse in the City of Toronto, I will summarize key aspects of my theoretical approach and research findings. I do this in a way that grounds my discussion on the relationships between agency, power, subjectivity, and desire, specifically how desires of racial Others to be not-raced and to belong in the diverse City have historical, political, and racial implications that further complicate the idea of agency as a matter of "choice." Importantly, when we consider agency as a matter of personal choice, we set ourselves up for dangerous comparative tropes that pit "resistant" subjects against "right kind of minority" subjects. What I have outlined in this book has hopefully begun to do away with these distinctions.

I will then turn to the work of a few scholars who write about agency, and then further their conceptualizations to situate agency within a local context, as an effect and affect of diversity discourse, with racial and spatial implications. In doing so, it becomes possible to also articulate the spatial dimensions of complicities and contradictions, or more specifically, their occlusions. Lastly, I pose key questions on agency so that we can continue to critically engage with the historical, social, and political forces of race, power, and diversity discourse in the City of Toronto, in spite of how they might shift.

Toronto the Good: Critical Insights

The research for this book has been guided by the central question of how race is reproduced and organized through diversity discourse in the City of Toronto. My intention was to explore how racialized City of Toronto staff understand and work with diversity in the City, but also to explicitly avoid making generalizations about their identities, "essences," and/or psyches. I sought instead to trace staff's positioning of themselves, their work, and their belonging in the City as being historically constituted, with reconstituting effects. To pursue this work, I drew on the methodological tenets of genealogy. This method enabled a reading of the interview transcripts against City of Toronto texts that named and/or offered policy directions on diversity, race, and/or racism, so that I could offer an understanding of subject positions taken up by racialized City staff as being *produced and productive,* within the confines of race and power. Specifically, I traced how the subjectivities of racialized City staff might incite and reproduce the racial norms of diversity discourse, through speech acts and texts. I also sought to identify any differences, similarities, tensions, and/or contradictions between interview transcripts and City texts, and how they might be indicative of the anxieties and regenerative aspects of diversity discourse in the City.

As Weedon (1997) explains, a genealogical method explores the relationships between power, knowledge, and discourse in the constitution of the subject, specifically how subjects' understandings of themselves and their worlds are historically, politically, and socially determined. Importantly, genealogy moves away from a humanistic approach that centres on the rationality, morality, freedom, and autonomy of the subject (Caldwell, 2007). It resists interpretations and reductions of the subject to an individual with a certain essence or character and, in the case of agency, to any who choose to fight against power because they possess the political awareness and "right" moral intentions to change the world.

As I have hopefully made visible in this book, commitments to social change based on personal, moral choices to "do the right thing" are grounded in and reproduce racial thinking, while further reinforcing individualistic notions of the Self as outside/against power. Even forms of resistance to diversity discourse in the City of Toronto can be traced to a reproduction and accommodation of its racializing norms and effects. Again, my methodological aim was not to seek out or divulge any "truth" about racialized City staff or other racial Others in the City, but to expose how power transforms and/or erases any historical, social, political, racial, and/or embodied schisms, to ensure the continuity of the racial norms of diversity discourse. I want to suggest here that morality – specifically the ability to choose to do and be the "right" thing – is but one way in which diversity discourse continues to occlude and reproduce racial norms in the City because it recentres the autonomous, free, and agentic individual subject, outside the bounds of power.

The theoretical concepts I describe in Chapter 2 provide the framework for understanding how negotiations of belonging for racial

Others in the City of Toronto are contained and reproduced by diversity discourse in racial terms, to recentre the autonomous, individual subject. I describe the space of the City of Toronto, diversity discourse, and belonging for racial Others as being *co-produced*. This means that the denials of racism and claims of leadership that make up the City as an exceptionally "diverse" space are co-produced with the racial terms of diversity discourse under which racial insider Others are included, become intelligible, and belong in the City as well as under which the occlusion and/or expulsion of racial other Others/outsiders and their claims becomes normalized.

Ahmed's (2002) theorization of racialization was pivotal to understanding this dynamic. My research revealed that the subject positions racialized City staff take up are produced and contained by diversity discourse to simultaneously refuse and re-inscribe racialization, in order to reinforce the boundaries between "us" (insider Others) and "them" (other Others/outsiders) as they negotiate their belonging in the City, a space where they would otherwise *not* belong. As I discovered, separations between "us" and "them" are made possible through the incitement of historical, racializing norms that abject and/or erase racial other Others/outsiders who make claims of racism in the space of the City. These norms are recirculated through speech acts and in City texts, to keep diversity discourse going.

Against this backdrop, I argue, the desires of racialized City staff and other racial Others in the City to be not-raced are hailed. Here, I offer that the hailing of the desires of racial Others to be not-raced in the diverse City is premised on the racial norms of diversity discourse that invite and authorize the autonomous, moral, and agentic insider Other subject in the City as one who belongs because they are *beyond the binds of race*. As I have shown, the racial terms of diversity discourse produce "insider" racial Others to take themselves up as exceptional, like no Other, and so on, to justify their belonging in an otherwise white space. Importantly, by encouraging these individual and/or agentic approaches to belonging in the City, it becomes more difficult to see how the contradictions and collusions that arise manifest and are occluded by subjectivizations of diversity discourse, race, and power. In other words, as an effect and affect of diversity discourse, the more autonomous and agentic the racial insider Other feels and/or claims to be, the more the reproduction of racialization and race becomes obscured in the City.

The separation between "us" and "them" as a negotiation of belonging for racial Others in the City is first taken up in Chapter 3, where I discuss how being exceptional is premised on conferring lack onto

racial other Others/outsiders. Although some staff's sense of themselves as exceptional was premised on their particular interpretations of
diversity, which intend to move diversity "beyond race" to effect social
and political change in the City, their interviews indicated moments of
tension that suggest a break with the coherency of their positionings.[1]
I use tensions here as opposed to contradictions because staff did not
actually see or take up these moments as contradictions *within themselves* in any real way (i.e., as effects of power/knowledge or the limits
of diversity discourse). Instead, these tensions were a result of institutional power over them and/or conceptualizations of diversity that
they *fight against*. It is in this chapter that I also begin to map a central
argument of this book: *the more critical/radical/progressive one identifies as
or claims to be, the more the potential for violence to be obscured.*

Tensions also occurred with staff who explicitly denied the existence of race and racism in the City. Although some staff were adamant that one's race does not matter or that racism does not exist in
the diverse City, in interviews there were moments where their denials of race/racism collided with their own embodied experiences of
being out of place and/or their observations that the City is indeed
a white space. These tense moments were effaced, however, as staff
justified their belonging in the City as exceptional individuals who
refused to rely on race and/or claims of racism, unlike other Oth-
ers/outsiders.[2] Importantly, staff's positioning in either case relied on
interpretations of diversity that they perceived to be *individually and
exceptionally authored*.

I foreground my analyses of the racial norms of diversity discourse
and being exceptional by drawing on City "diversity" texts. I show how
staff who described their interpretations of diversity as exceptional,
individually authored, and/or autonomous were in fact drawing on
and reproducing the historical, racial norms of diversity discourse that
had been circulating in City texts for decades, particularly the essence
of racial *lack*. In City texts, racial claims in the diverse City were repeatedly reframed and/or occluded through reproducing the racial "outsider" figure who simply lacked the proper education, language, culture, skills, and knowledge needed to participate in the City. In this, the
City is also reproduced as an exceptional space where there is no racism. I argue in this chapter that staff subjectivities are hailed, produced,
and contained by diversity discourse to recirculate and then set themselves apart from these norms and, by extension, "outsider" figures and
their racial claims, thus legitimizing staff's desires and belonging in the
diverse City as *not-raced*. In interviews and in City texts, the reproduction, effects, and affects of the racial norms of diversity discourse were

glossed over and/or made irrelevant because of the various forms of being exceptional that they inspire.

It is important that we also discuss how being exceptional reeks of neoliberalism and individualism. Both Stuart Hall (2017) and Wendy Brown (2019) write that the logics of capitalism and morality converge and have been re-enlivened through neoliberalism where, for example, individual success, recognition, and reward is believed to come through hard work, resilience, and a heightened sense of responsibility. While some might be aware or even hypercritical of this "entrepreneurial" narrative, Brown is quick to remind us, drawing on Foucault's notion of governmentality, of how we conduct ourselves in ways that internalize, align with, and refashion the logics of neoliberalism, to ensure its continuity. In short, the binaries are not as rigid as we think. Hall (1988) draws us a very clear picture of what this looks like in the United Kingdom:[3]

> [M]ake no mistake, a tiny bit of all of us is also somewhere inside the Thatcherite project. Of course, we're all one hundred per cent committed. But every now and then – Saturday mornings, perhaps, just before the demonstration – we go to Sainsbury's and we're just a tiny bit of a Thatcherite subject. (p. 165)

Many of us, especially those of us engulfed in our critical hazes, can miss how being exceptional is, in reality, not exceptional in the least. We are produced to see ourselves as exceptional individuals, again, perhaps at the expense of larger social and political transformation, community-building, and solidarity. In this way (and in many others), neoliberal rationalities are hardly confined to the "Right."

This book has also shown how neoliberal rationalities govern our "conduct" as *heroic* subjects. Davies (1991) writes that the humanist approach to agency positions the individual as one "who stands out of the collective, against the pressures of society ... heroes who engage in difficult tasks, as people who we might become" (p. 42). Chapter 3 begins to illuminate how this self-proclaimed "hero" who stands outside of the collective in the diverse City can indeed take on many forms. Nevertheless, the racial hailing and positionings of Others in the diverse City centre on their being autonomous, heroic, and moral individuals outside the bounds of race and power to preclude further probing or analyses of moments of tension, contradiction, and collusion, in speech acts and/or in texts. Although probing of these tensions, contradictions, and collusions might indicate the failure of diversity discourse to fully encapsulate the speaking and writing subject, their occlusions and/

or reconciliations also demonstrate the exceedingly powerful effects and affects of diversity discourse. I have also shown how the heroic "exceptional" positionings in the diverse City and the separations thus implied ("us" versus "them") can, as Ahmed (2012) suggests, defend against complicity.[4]

In Chapter 4, the heroic individual subject again emerges, this time having "specialized knowledge" of racialized groups that props up the insider Other's unique position and abilities to effect change in the City. I show how the racial terms under which this specialized knowledge is articulated and taken up are obscured from view, as are insider Others' collusions with the familiar racial norms of diversity discourse, because diversity sets up, produces, and grants subjectivity and belonging under the conditions that one knows and is also *unlike* other racial Others. I argue in this chapter that the possession and dissemination of specialized knowledge brings racial insider Others in the City – as "knowers" – into close(r) proximity to the white male somatic norm while further naturalizing the white male somatic norm in the City as the ultimate bearer of knowledge and truth.

I also argued that this specialized knowledge of racialized communities undergirds the morality of racial Others like no Other and the somatic norm. Staff who took up the position of having specialized knowledge articulated how they sought social and/or political change *for "them"* (outsiders). In fact, this was also the premise for the formation and racial membership of the City's Committees seeking to combat racism and racial discrimination, including the Toronto Mayor's Committee on Community and Race Relations: select racial Others were invited and included in the City because they were uniquely positioned to help "translate" the claims of racial other Others/outsiders. Staff and other racial insider Others are thus invited into and reproduce heroic, moral, and individual subject positionings by being like no Other, again, with racializing effects that ultimately keep racial other Others and their racial claims firmly outside the City. These racializing effects are further entrenched as racial insider Others produced like no Other negotiate and in some cases teeter on the edge of the race/civility/belonging paradigm in the otherwise white space of the diverse City, continuously drawing on racial stereotypes to plant themselves in close(r) proximity to the somatic figure, as like no other racial Other and ultimately, as not-raced. In doing so, racial insiders like no Other re-constitute, de-historicize, and occlude the colonial imperatives of diversity discourse that grant and refuse civility and belonging for racial Others in the City on the basis of proximity to the somatic norm. Here, we might consider how racial insider Others like no Other taking up heroic and moral positionings *is a direct reflection of their proximity*.

Chapter 5 delves into the racial norms of diversity discourse that are invited and reproduced through consultation with racial Others in the City of Toronto. Again, the impetus for racialized City staff to push for more consultation with racial Others was their positionings as agentic subjects who sought to transform the City's diversity policies and practices and effect institutional change. However, as City texts revealed, the presence and participation of "consulted" racial Others is repeatedly commodified to demonstrate and recirculate the City's leadership on addressing racism and diversity issues and increasing the democratic participation of racialized groups. Although Others' experiences of racism can be traced in City "consultation" texts, under the racial norms of diversity, these experiences are continuously reframed and/or erased to reinforce claims of inclusion and progress that the City of Toronto is known for. My analyses suggest that the idealization of democracy and racial inclusion, incited into and reproduced through diversity discourse, is refracted through racial insider Others' sense of themselves as agentic as well as their desires to be not-raced and to belong in the City, as insider Others who *have the capacity bring racial other Others in*. I argue in this chapter that bringing other Others in through consultation is precisely what racial insider Others have been produced to do.

Therefore can anything ever really change in the City of Toronto, given the omnipresence of diversity discourse, race, and power and that racial insiders are always, in some way, complicit?

On the Problem of Agency

The true focus of revolutionary change is never merely the oppressive situation which we seek to escape, but that piece of the oppressor which is planted deep within each of us, and which knows only the oppressor's tactics, the oppressor's relationships.

Audre Lorde (1984, p. 123)

Audre Lorde (1984) reminds us of perhaps the most important part of justice work: owning how we might stand in the way of it. Parker (2012) writes that some feminist theorists and activists critique Foucault's understanding of agency, arguing that their strategies to resist and undo sexism, patriarchy, and power are inseparable from resisting complicity with patriarchal ideals. However, what is often obscured in feminist work equating agency with resisting complicity with patriarchy are the

neocolonial, Western, Eurocentric, and appropriating terms that undergird such resistance and legitimize the universalization of whiteness,
alongside and *through* the exoticization and objectification of "Others."
Parker thus situates agency within a politics of location, specifically an
awareness and refusal of complicities with *all* subject/Other relations.
A politics of location makes visible the silences, erasures, and appropri-
ations that are produced and reinforced by making the subject, knowledge, and subjection in Western, imperial, raced, classed, gendered,
heteronormative, and/or nationalist terms. This approach to agency
centralizes complicities within relations of power and also contextual-
izes modes of internalized oppression within relations and subjectivizations of power, so that they are no longer conceived of as an inherent
"weakness" of the individual, free subject.

Here, I take up Parker's insights into agency to again suggest that the
illumination of and reckoning with contradictions and complicities with
discourse, race, and power makes it possible to expose the effects and
affects of diversity discourse in the City of Toronto, invisibilized by whatever ideas we are produced to have about ourselves. Through Parker's
politics of location (vis-à-vis complicity with subject/Other relations),
we can begin to understand how subjectivity, intelligibility, articulation,
and belonging of racial insider Others in the diverse City are authorized
against the racialization, abjection, and/or exclusion of racial other Oth-
ers/outsiders. In this book I have extended Parker's politics of location
to suggest that separations of "us" and "them," authorized through the
reproduction of racialization, abjection, and/or exclusion of racial other
Others/outsiders, also attend to racial insider Others' desires to be not-
raced and to resolve – however temporarily – their embodied experiences
of being out of place. Nevertheless, attention to subject/Other complicities brings to the fore how racial insider Others in the City of Toronto are
produced under the racial norms of diversity discourse to perform and
embody individuality and coherency of the Self. The point that I have
hopefully made in this book is that the binaries of "us and "them" that
make up racial insider Others as individual, coherent subjects are in fact
less rigid and totalizing than they appear. By illuminating the fractures
of the coherent individual subject, it becomes possible to understand the
racial, colonial anxieties of diversity discourse, as well as how and under
what conditions they are repeated and subverted in the present.

On Complicity and the Politics of Admission

Chapter 1 detailed how I arrived at my central research question:
through reflecting upon my years as former political staff in the City of
Toronto, specifically as a racial insider Other who drew upon discourses

of diversity, agency, and resistance to *personally* invoke and sustain an anti-racist agenda in the City. I was hell-bent on "doing diversity differently." During my research, I began to see how racial Others in the City accessed similar agentic subject positions, whereby their actions, feelings, and desires became intimately connected with and reflected individualized, autonomous, and essential notions of the Self, rather than constituted by and through diversity discourse.

There is a deeper story here, however. In the last moments of my PhD defence, where I presented the research underpinning this book, I was asked a poignant question: "Have you thought about how your work will be taken up *as diversity work*?" I froze. Despite my interventions on diversity discourse and complicity, I had not examined how the academic work that I had pursued for seven years was also complicit with the racializing conventions and norms I sought to expose. I thought I was "doing diversity differently," *again*. I could not see – or perhaps refused to engage with – how my critical research project could in fact keep the diversity project going. As a self-proclaimed critical scholar in the academy, I was absolutely complicit in keeping diversity alive. I still am.

So what then do these admissions of complicity actually *do*? An approach to agency and diversity discourse that makes complicities and contradictions visible has its concerns. Acknowledgment of complicities and contradictions with diversity discourse, race, and power could very well become wielded as an *apparatus* of power, simply by taking up and reproducing positioning(s) as the "truly ethical" racial insider Other. This critique could similarly be leveraged against the establishment of critical whiteness studies and alike in academic institutions across the globe. White scholars who conceive of themselves as being "ethically aware" of their racial privilege and who identify collusions with whiteness might actually reinforce and reproduce their own whiteness and innocence, as well as the whiteness and innocence of the institution. This paradox also resonates with Ahmed's (2006) observations on the politics of admission, specifically that institutional and individual admissions to being racist are in themselves seen as acts of doing good and of being anti-racist. In the City of Toronto, the presence of "ethically responsible" racial subjects could also be taken up by the institution to demonstrate and reinforce the City's *increased* commitment to and leadership on addressing race and diversity. From my personal experience in the City, I can say that this has often been the case.

However, framing agency as "good" versus "bad," resistance versus complicity, again sets up the totalitarian binaries that reinforce and reproduce the idea of the agentic, free, and rational individual,

outside the binds of race and power. Instead, I argue that by dili-
gently making visible the complicities with power in tandem with
the *contradictions* that are effaced in recognizing these complicities,[5] it
becomes possible to increasingly interrogate and destabilize totalized
subjectivities – i.e., the "critical scholar," the "activist-academic," or
even the "activist" – and then work towards a greater accountability
to act(ion). The recognition of complicities and contradictions is thus
to "engage with the unnatural" (Butler, 2011, p. 190) and to engage
with what might seem and feel *impossible*, on a psychic level. This can
be a complex, constantly evolving, intensely reflective and uncomfort-
able process – especially now, where neoliberal, individual ideas of
ourselves as famed academics/activists/heroes are especially encouraged. But we should not and cannot stop at discomfort. As Caldwell
(2007) explains, an approach to agency that destabilizes the coherence
of the individual subject shifts the focus from moral or political tasks
to make a difference, to an ability "to *act otherwise*" (p. 789). In this
vein, the confluence of discourse of diversity, race, and power and
the confrontation of its contradictions and collusions also compels a
constant negotiation with the (non-totalized) Self to act from a place
of awareness and subversion of racial norms, *in ways that also risk our
Selves*.[6]

I am not suggesting that by acting in greater variation, subversion,
and accountability, we can expect a complete elimination of race,
power, diversity discourse, and/or its future iterations, in the City of
Toronto and beyond. Instead, I propose that these subversive acts have,
as Butler (2011) also implies, the potential to disrupt conventional rep-
etitions of racializing norms and to *reveal* the failure of discourse, race,
and power to "ever fully legislate or contain their own ideals" (p. 237).
Although this constant revealing, undoing, and acting otherwise can be
quite challenging, exhausting, risky, and perhaps even painful, it also
has the potential to be liberating – not only for ourselves, but also in the
greater pursuit of social justice.

Revisiting Racial Inclusion

Drawing on Black anti-colonial thinkers C.L.R. James, W.E.B. Du Bois,
Franz Fanon, Cedric Robinson, Walter Rodney, and others, Lowe
(2015) brilliantly outlines how racial representation and inclusion
tropes keep liberal narratives – hinging on promises of universal freedom, subjectivity, humanity, personhood, and moral law – intact.
Here, racial difference and dehumanization can constitute "progressive" (read: Eurocentric) historical developments and interventions;

the progression of a universal humanity, ethical reasoning subject, freedom, and/or liberal-democratic state, for example, occurs through *negation and/or subsumption.*[7] In *The Black Jacobins*, C.L.R. James exposes negation of the antislavery revolution in Haiti in particular in Hegel's dialectic and Western Marxism (to name a few), both of which subscribe to teleological narratives of history and progress inherent to the Western, European tradition. Lowe summarizes one of the main points of James's work:

> The contradiction of master and slave was the dynamic impulse of historical progress, but for James, the *sublation* of contradiction into the European state form[8] was insufficient to bring an end to the dehumanization of slavery; conciliation could not be achieved by mere inclusion of the enslaved into French history or civil society, or by the replacement of the colonizer by the native bourgeoisie. *The Black Jacobins* is the epic history of the slaves demanding that the entire social structure be changed from the bottom up, that the society be established on new foundations. (p. 157)

Importantly, James's work on the Haitian revolution not only destabilizes historical narratives that make up the Western tradition, it *exceeds* them.

Lowe also discusses W.E.B. Du Bois's *Black Reconstruction*, specifically his interrogation of the formal abolition of slavery in the US South as being foundational to the racial divisions of labour that continue to uphold the United States as simultaneously capitalist and liberal-democratic:

> In 1935, Du Bois captured the way in which the liberal promises of humanitarian "abolition" and "emancipation" did not end slavery, but enabled the triumph of U.S. capitalist industry that inaugurated instead the expansion of capitalism globally, permitting the "re-enslavement" of labor linking Africa, Asia, and the Americas: "Within the very echo of that philanthropy which had abolished the slave trade, was beginning a new industrial slavery of black and brown and yellow workers in Africa and Asia." (p. 169)

Why do I draw on these works now? Because they compel us to think not only about how racial negation and/or subsumption are productive, but also how negation might be considered "repaired," even *excised*, through some form of racial representation and inclusion in liberal apparatuses, e.g., to "enrich" the traditional Western literary canon, or in the case of the liberal-democratic state, granting citizenship and civil rights to freed slaves, signifying the formal end of racial inequality – just enough (and just in time) to recover liberal stakes in universal humanity, freedom, and progress, anxiously provoked by discursive and material spaces of war across the globe.[9] James's work exposes the racist, colonial foundations undergirding and also limiting Western narratives of progress and freedom, and in doing so, offers up a more expansive imagining of revolutionary change, *beyond inclusion and incorporation into the same*. Du Bois teaches us that the recovery of liberal democracies through racial inclusion in the state is also precisely when and how race manifests and thrives, in other forms, in other ways, obscured by a renewed liberal innocence.[10]

Ferreira da Silva (2007) echoes these principles in her brilliant critique of theories of race that reconstitute Self/Other relations and claim "that racial emancipation comes about when the (juridical and economic) inclusion of the racial others and their voices (historical and cultural representations) finally realizes universality" (p. 154). For Ferreira da Silva, pursuit of the logics of exclusion can become invested in and focused on narratives of injury and repair, rather than on how and why the state legitimizes and authorizes the reproduction of racial subjugation. The historical, moral ascription of racial and cultural difference – or raciality, as Ferreira da Silva names it – (re-)produces raced bodies as well as the racial terms under which the state engages with those bodies, in the interests of the self-preservation of the state and its laws that protect the ethical subject. The legitimacy of the state's actions is thus "always already given – in exteriority" through raciality (Ferreira da Silva, 2014, p. 160). Ferreira da Silva is saying, and I agree, that state actions and laws do not produce raciality; rather, raciality produces the actions and laws of the state. This is what calls for more inclusive democracies fail to recognize: raciality necessitates racial exclusion, abjection, even violence.

The paradoxes of racial representation and inclusion are that the violences of diversity and other institutionalized discourses could not exist without the inclusion of racial Others and/or racial claims. Put simply, institutional racism thrives through racial inclusion.[11] But does this mean, then, that we must refuse racial representation and inclusion altogether? The answer is complex and can often be specific to time, site, and situation. What is clear, however, is that agency and resistance in the context of diversity discourse and its future iterations – whatever they might be, in the City of Toronto and beyond – cannot remain grounded in and hopeful about the work that racial insider Others can do in order for themselves and other racial Others to *be and feel included*. Following Ferreira da Silva's critical interventions, I suggest that we move away from seeing agency and resistance solely in terms of achieving greater racial inclusion, and instead investigate points of agency and resistance as a critical interrogation of *legitimacy*; that is, the role of institutions in always-already legitimizing exteriority and violence (via diversity and other discourses) to reinscribe their authority and self-determination. What happens when we refuse processes and policies of inclusion into the same, and instead initiate critical interventions in how, why, and under what terms racial Others are always-already constituted, by the state, the academy, and other institutional spaces, via exteriority? What if questions turned to what racial "insider Others" are always-already *doing* for diversity and other discourses, instead of what they might *do* to and with them?

This book has traced and rendered visible the racial norms that are incited into and by diversity discourse, to reproduce race in the City of Toronto, in the present. I have argued that these norms have remained largely unquestioned because of their historical production and familiarity, exacerbated by how they have been recirculated and normalized through texts and speech acts. This book has also begun to expose how diversity discourse narrows intelligibility, articulation, and belonging of racial Others in racial(izing) terms that simultaneously hail their desires to be not-raced and to belong in the City, a space that is at once "diverse" and inherently meant for the white, upper/middle-class male somatic norm. I argue that the question of what diversity and other discourses "do" must continue to attend to and reveal their racial norms, particularly how they bend and shift in current local contexts to constitute and be constituted by the racial subjectivities, desires, and negotiations of belonging of racial insider Others in institutional settings across the globe.

At the very least, this book might make it more difficult to continue the same diversity agenda and attendant racial practices that have been recirculating over the past almost fifty years – practices that have ultimately rendered racial Others out of place in the City of Toronto because they *lack*, or that have reframed and then erased their racial claims from the City's landscape. My hope is that this book also invites us as racial insider Others to engage in a thorough questioning, undoing, and then redefining of how and under what terms agency and belonging in institutional spaces can co-exist within the ongoing discursive, material, and psychic constraints that repeatedly invite us to perform and act *as heroic individuals*. In this vein, it is crucial that we begin and/or continue to fiercely engage and contend with our own complicities and contradictions, and work toward greater accountability to act, beyond our Selves, subjectivities, and degrees of belonging, always with the firm understanding that no matter what we do or who we think we are, *there is no innocent space.*

Notes

1. The Diversification of Diversity

1 Since 2015 there have been numerous other billboards with messages about diversity or anti-racism being about white genocide or "anti-white," including on university campuses. Many (but not all) are connected to the "White Genocide Project."

2 I will refer to Toronto's municipal government in this book as the "City of Toronto," or "City." Otherwise, "city" or simply "Toronto" refers to the metropolitan/urban space, as in where people live. It is my contention that the former ("City of Toronto" or "City") plays a pivotal role in how the latter ("city" or "Toronto") is taken up as the "most diverse," "post-racial," etc., in local, national, and international contexts.

3 See above.

4 See, e.g., the *2015–2018 City of Toronto Strategic Plan* and City of Toronto motto "Diversity Our Strength" (City of Toronto, n.d.-a).

5 Puwar (2001) refers to the somatic norm in her work as "the corporeal imagination of power as naturalised in the body of white, male, upper/middle class bodies" (p. 652).

6 Puwar describes how "disorientation" and "infantilization" are often reactions to racial Others in the British senior civil service.

7 Several feminist race scholars have taken up the exact term "out of place," including Mohanram (1999), Puwar (2004), Ahmed (2012). It is important to note that others have developed the *idea* of being out of place, both in relation to space and as a racial Other. See, for example, Fanon (1952).

8 Lowe additionally refers to works by C.L.R. James, W.E.B. Du Bois, Franz Fanon, Cedric Robinson, Walter Rodney, and other Black anti-colonial thinkers to trace what those alternative accounts were.

9 Ferreira da Silva (2015) writes this as "missing": "Why does Foucault's description of the same transformations, and his 'theory of domination' as understood in relation to modern through, *miss* the connection?" (p. 97).

10 I am thinking here of a consultation meeting I attended in 2002, as part of the City of Toronto's (2003a) *Plan of Action for the Elimination of Racism and Discrimination*. As participants painfully recounted their experiences of racism in Toronto, I witnessed several white women in the audience hold their chests, shake their heads, or hold back tears, but also almost breathe collective sighs of relief that the pain they were witnessing *was not theirs*. This was, to me, evidence of what Farley (1997) calls "race-pleasure." I pick this theme up again in Chapter 5, on consultation.

11 I discussed the importance of understanding the seductive power of white supremacy in more detail on *The Dr. Vibe Show*, alongside U.S.-based author and activist LeRon Barton (see Barton & Almeida, 2020). Our episode – "White Supremacy and the Exception to the Rule" – attempted to unpack (in addition to other examples) the increase in numbers of Black, Latino, and Asian people who voted for Donald Trump in the 2020 U.S. Presidential Election. We used statistics provided by Gramlich (2020) from the Pew Research Center, and others, to support our conversation.

12 I used "multicultural" after finding a link between it and diversity in texts describing the former City's Multicultural Access Program.

13 Some also reference the East York Multicultural and Race Relations Coordinating Committee but my search was limited to the former municipality of the City of Toronto.

14 In 1980 the term "diversity" also appears in a Toronto Firefighters' training manual, which denotes the importance of "respecting diversity." I also first saw the term "diversity management" in a report entitled, *Summary of Corporate Training on Multicultural and Race Relations* (City of Toronto, 1990b, p. 12.147).

15 Archives staff explained that there are significant gaps in coverage, particularly in the 1980s and 1990s, hence my two-phase search.

16 The question of who is authoring "performative" City texts (and "performative" commitments) also presumes not only a context in which racial Others struggle against and/or under a regime in which the "change" or progress they seek is limited, but also where only white and/or "right kind of minority" staff write such less-than-critical texts. Again, I want to do away with drawing such firm distinctions because they are dangerously simplistic.

17 Admittedly, my foray into the idea of diversity as the reproduction of racial norms began with reading City texts that unabashedly covered over claims of racism with performative statements, in tandem with select interview transcripts that detailed staff refusing the possibilities of racism

in the City. This exploration expanded, however, once I began to think about how diversity also invites and produces the heroic, individual-resistant subject via the reproduction of racial norms. This "expansion" was in large part because of my choice of methodology, specifically the concept of historical "truths" and how they are reproduced through texts and speech acts.

I describe how this subject(ivity) is linked to the reproduction of race (and as a function of maintaining the space of the "diverse" City) in Chapter 3, and then continue to develop this line of thinking throughout the rest of the book.

18 I have included some of the materials from the original "Good Sell" theme in Chapter 2 and Chapter 5, to showcase how commodification and erasure also happen when opportunities to market the City on a national and/or international scale occur. Some of the content of two remaining themes, "Diversity as Morality" and "Doing Diversity" have been interspersed throughout the book.

19 Governmentality (Foucault, 1979) was also helpful here – how subjects internalize, rationalize, and fulfil techniques of state power; a "government of the Self" (Rose et al., 2009, p. 10). I expand on the idea of governmentality in Chapter 2, to again dispel any view of power as "top down" and to further complicate the idea that belonging is granted in the City to "specific kinds" of racial Others.

2. Theoretical Concepts

1 Abu-Laban and Gabriel (2002) and Catungal and Leslie (2009), for example, argue that diversity logics commodify, market, and bill ethno-racial difference as trade-enhancing. Similarly, Jordan and Weedon (2015) describe how, in the age of diversity and cultural pluralism, racial Others have become "highly profitable commodities" (p. 155). For Shaw (2007), diversity is a consumable product of whiteness, rather than a range of types of people, as it seems to suggest. Only those who have the class, cash, and right ethnicity can enjoy the rewards and benefits of "ethnic" diversity. Smith (2010) also writes that diversity draws directly on corporate logic, market-based strategies, and the achievement of goals and standards alongside the management and containment of internal differences. The new governing mentality under late capitalism requires that "these differences be ironed out and 'integrated'" (p. 47). However, Croucher (1997) and others argue that, because the City of Toronto relies heavily on its image as a "diverse" city of multiple languages, cultures, and positive ethnic relations to compete effectively in the global marketplace, any struggles based on race and class are effectively written out of the historical and political space of the city. My theorization of

diversity in the City of Toronto complicates this assumption, specifically that the success and re-circulation of diversity rhetoric depends on and necessitates the exclusion/expulsion of racism.

2 I am reminded here of Ahmed's (2012) assertion that institutional statements of commitment are "non-performative" (p. 117). Through their reproduction and circulation, these institutional statements of commitment to "achieve" diversity goals and/or initiatives work to reaffirm the "goodness" of the institution, while concealing "the failure of that document to do anything" (Ahmed, 2012, p. 97).

3. Being Exceptional

1 For Hook, there must be a psychoanalytic dimension of human motivation (passion, attachments, investments) involved in analyses of power and subjectivity, which account for the shifting manifestations, expressions, and/or disruptions between disciplinary power and individual conduct.

2 A citizen committee of 12 struck by Mayor Art Eggleton in 1981 to help the City "deal with problems concerning the visible minority community, especially racism" (City of Toronto, 1981a, p. 1054).

3 In City texts there is a historical conflation of racialized and immigrant, which then signals that a lack of "Canadian" skills is the reason for the under-representation of racialized employees in the City. I discuss examples of these texts throughout the book.

4 Report/Work Plan to the City's Executive Committee, from the Executive Director, Social Development, Finance and Administration, and General Manager, Toronto Employment and Social Services.

5 See City of Toronto (2017d) for a full list of recommendations.

6 This is also a question, I think, of the larger forces and events – social, political, economic, local, national, international, and so on – that inspire shifts in how racism is defined, articulated, and taken up, when and by whom. In this vein, it is worth considering how these relatively isolated exceptional moments (and the inclusion of exceptional subjects that create them) are not necessarily tied to increased action on racism in the City, at least not without the accountability demands and other effects emanating from larger forces. Also key here is that being exceptional in the City and beyond invites and works through *isolation*, perhaps at the expense of building collective spaces and action.

7 In response to the onslaught of hate crime related to the heightened presence of the Ku Klux Klan in Toronto, the former Municipality of Metropolitan Toronto established the annual Access and Equity Grant Program, to "promote respect and value for the City's ethno-racial communities and to strengthen positive race relations in the

City" (City of Toronto, 2000a, p. 2). Each year that the City (and/or its former municipalities) has allocated grants to not-for-profit community organizations so that *they* may "advocate for the removal of legislative and institutional barriers" (p. 4), reports describe *the City* as leading in equity and "creating a positive and welcoming environment for Toronto's diverse communities" (p. 2), because it partially funds these organizations.

8 See *Diversity and Positive Workplace Strategy* (City of Toronto, 2009a) for definitions of inclusion specific to working in the City.

9 The word "inclusion" also appears in reference to the annual Access and Equity Grant Program, developed in 1980 to help fund community organizations that "promote respect and value for Toronto's multicultural and multiracial character" (City of Toronto, 2001c, p. 3) and seek to improve access to services and promote civic participation. City texts repeatedly refer to the program as a way to demonstrate the City's leadership in "encouraging the inclusion and participation of marginalized communities in the City" (p. 3). However, these texts do not refer to racism *in the City specifically.*

4. Being Like No Other

1 In December 1992 Toronto police set up their first hate crimes unit to investigate acts of racist violence and vandalism at the hands of white supremacist groups, as well as the growing spread of hate propaganda. At the time, Zundel's Holocaust denial materials made up the largest source of hate propaganda in Toronto (City of Toronto, 1993b).

2 Also see Mohanram (1999) and Puwar (2004) for references to raced and gendered bodies being "out of place."

3 I use "event" in Foucauldian terms, to trace strategies, reversals, erasures, plays of force, blockages, and continuities that make up diversity discourse and its appearance as normative and linear.

4 I would also argue that the perception of anger is authorized through colonial and racial thinking, to mark uncivilized racial bodies.

5 Incidentally, in a meeting of Council on 28 October 1998, in the process of deciding the final makeup of City's coat of arms, Councillor Kelly requested that the City's motto "Diversity Our Strength" be replaced by "*Civility* Our Strength" (City of Toronto, 1998a, p. 1815).

6 Racism in the City was also identified as a problem during the consultation with ethnic groups. In the City's official list of issues recorded from the consultations, racism shows up as "discrimination" and "perceived racial overtones" in the City (City of Toronto, 1990b, p. 155).

7 Ethnic groups were Black, South Asian, Chinese, Portuguese, and Filipino. Although the Committee may have done consultations by ethnic group in some strategic way, the recommendations coming out of the consultations

also further substantiated the re-framing of racism as stemming from differences of language and culture. They included translation of City materials in several languages, increasing employee awareness of the cultural, linguistic, and religious needs of minority groups, better outreach to ethnic media outlets, and increasing representation of racial and ethnic groups in the City's workforce to meet the needs of various groups.

8 One of the City's immediate responses to issues of access was to also initiate City-wide, multi-day trainings for staff from various departments, which was called Corporate Training on Multicultural and Race Relations. These trainings were called "Diversity in the Workplace" (Buildings & Inspections Department), "Cultures" and "Managing and Working with Diversity" (Finance Department), and "Managing Diversity" (Fire Department), to name a few (City of Toronto, 1990c, p. 147–48).

9 For example, in the "Multicultural Access to City Services" report, Mayor Eggleton praised the Toronto Mayor's Committee for using whatever means necessary – "moral suasion, advocacy, or direct action – to try to ensure that everyone in this community has equal access to housing, to government services, to employment" (City of Toronto, 1990a, p. 5).

10 They have all been "advisory" committees, formed to provide advice to the Mayor and/or City Council.

11 These would be the Race and Ethnic Relations Committee and the Aboriginal Affairs Committee, without taking into account intersecting identities that might also elicit experiences of racism in the other three Committees. It is also worth noting that the original recommendation of the Task Force was that *seven* Committees be created. The recommended Racial Minorities, Ethno-cultural and Multi-faith Issues, and Immigrant and Refugee Issues Committees were collapsed into one Race and Ethnic Relations Committee.

12 Although Councillor Mihevc does not navigate the same desires to be not-raced and to transgress racial lines that reinforce racialized staff's assertions that they can do diversity differently, I would suggest that what links Councillor Mihevc's assertion and staff's desires is that diversity can somehow be mobilized to move beyond race.

13 The point I want to stress here is that both the fear of being the stereotype and the containment of that fear are necessary to occlude the production of racial Others like no Other in the diverse City.

14 By "diversity strategies" I mean historical moves that the City has made and repeated, to ensure the reproduction and occlusion of race.

5. Being Through Consultation

1 See, e.g., Saloojee (2003) and Zhuang (2018), who argue that more engagement with racial Others (via consultation) is needed to make the City truly diverse, equitable, and/or anti-racist.

2 See, e.g., City of Toronto (2009b), which contains strong language, i.e., the Aboriginal community "as the original peoples of this land" (p. 6), but then recommends "diversity and cultural competency training" for all service members: "Cultural competency means the ability to interact skillfully with people of different cultures … knowledge of different cultural practices and world views, the possession of cross-cultural skills" (p. 7).

3 Paschel refers to this as participating "in a dance of ritualized participation" (Meyers, 1993, as cited in Paschel, 2016, p. 200), and in the case of Colombia, argues that it was instrumental in the "unmaking of black rights and policies" (p. 218).

4 Other issues of anti-Black racism in the City have been identified and were also spelled out in the extensive consultation leading up to the City's *Interim Toronto Action Plan to Confront Anti-Black Racism* (City of Toronto, 2017b).

5 See, e.g., Beattie (2017) and Nasser (2017).

6 Farley quotes Fanon here: "[W]herever he goes, the Negro remains a Negro" (Farley, 1997, p. 474).

6. On Diversity Discourse and the Problem of Agency

1 These were contradictions that were illuminated in interviews with racialized City staff, which very few paused to think through. Those who did, did so very briefly. For example, staff separated themselves from others in and outside the City ("them") by indicating that their definitions of diversity include multiple identities and/or intersections of race, class, gender, sexual orientation, age, religion, and so on. However, in our interviews, they discussed how when they use the term in the City, or write it in reports, they generally mean race. Only one interviewee takes a brief moment to reflect on this: "I've not thought about that until this second…"

2 See "not seeing" section in Chapter 3 for further discussion.

3 In the British context and the reign of ultra-conservative former prime minister Margaret Thatcher in particular. Hall writes that the root of the success of Thatcherism was that "[i]t is a project – this confuses the Left no end – which is, simultaneously, regressive and progressive" (Hall 1988, p. 166).

4 Ahmed (2012) writes that "the presumption of our own criticality can be a way of protecting ourselves from complicity" (p. 5). I show a different kind of binary thinking ("us" versus "them") that is instead explicitly racial and spatial.

5 For example, the recognition of complicities effects (and obscures) the desires to become "good" and a race to innocence, which might further incite a consolidation of the Self and thus complicity with racial thinking.

6 Butler (1990) calls agency "subversive repetition" (p. 188): to intervene, denaturalize, destabilize, and contest the repetition of "traditional" gender norms via engaging the "unnatural" (p. 190). I would argue that contesting and subverting gender norms in this way does not necessarily displace gender/heteronormativity, but instead questions its very authority.

7 Lowe draws on Black anti-colonial thinkers such as W.E.B. Du Bois, C.L.R. James, Franz Fanon, Cedric Robinson, and others who challenge the supremacy of European narratives of industry, progress, and capital in the evolution of the modern world via tracing their negation of Africa (externalized as "pre-modern") and Black slaves (positioned in Marxism as "precapitalist" – see Lowe, 2015, p. 149) as well as the continued dehumanization of Black and Indigenous peoples, dispossession of land, and labour and exploitation of colonized peoples. Robinson argues that race and racial difference have always been an inherent organizing force in/of capitalism, hence his term "racial capitalism" (Lowe, 2015, p. 150). Other non-European worlds (i.e., Asia, Arab, Muslim) are subsumed under European teleological narratives of development as backwards, inferior, undeveloped, and other colonial tropes that essentially prevent their incorporation/participation in universal humanity, progress, and freedom.

8 For instance the sublation of the master-slave dialectic inevitably leading to the progress, triumph, and redemption of humanity.

9 Lowe also brilliantly traces the negation and erasure of the roles of the slave revolution and Pan-African anti-colonial movements in numerous European historians' works on revolutionary thought, capitalism, democracy, and/or freedom.

10 In the context of the Canadian nation state, Bannerji (1997) also teaches us that the racial Other is written into the discourse of the liberal-democratic, multicultural, diverse nation as a condition of liberal transcendence, not as an outcome of it.

11 I argue exactly this in Almeida (2021).

References

Abu-Laban, Y., & Gabriel, C. (2002). *Selling diversity: Immigration, multiculturalism, employment equity, and globalization*. University of Toronto Press.

Ahmadi, D. (2018). Is diversity our strength? An analysis of the facts and fancies of diversity in Toronto. *City, Culture and Society, 13*, 64–72. https://doi.org/10.1016/j.ccs.2017.11.002

Ahmadi, D., & Tasan-Kok, T. (2013). *Assessment of urban policies in Canada*. Research Report submitted to European Commission. Faculty of Architecture and the Built Environment, Delft University of Technology.

Ahmed, S. (2000). *Strange encounters: Embodied others in post-coloniality*. Routledge.

Ahmed, S. (2002). Racialized bodies. In M. Evans & E. Lee (Eds.), *Real bodies: A sociological Introduction* (pp. 46–63). Palgrave.

Ahmed, S. (2004). Affective economies. *Social Text, 22*(2), 117–39. https://doi.org/10.1215/01642472-22-2_79-117

Ahmed, S. (2006). The nonperformativity of antiracism. *Meridians, 7*(1), 104–26.

Ahmed, S. (2007). The language of diversity. *Ethnic and Racial Studies, 30*(2), 235–56. https://doi.org/10.1080/01419870601143927

Ahmed, S. (2012). *On being included: Racism and diversity in institutional life*. Duke University Press.

Ahmed, S. (2019, 22 July). Why complain? *feministkilljoys*. https://feministkilljoys.com/2019/07/22/why-complain/

Ahmed, S. (2021, 22 March). *Courageous conversations: Complaint, diversity and other hostile environments* [Video]. Courageous speaker series, University of Calgary. YouTube. https://youtu.be/dy4ZYnJ6jQk

Almeida, S. (2016). *Theorizing the local: Diversity, race, and belonging in the City of Toronto* [Unpublished doctoral dissertation]. York University.

Almeida, S. (2018, 14 January). *On being exceptional: The trap of thinking we can do (and be) diversity "differently."* Media Diversified. https://mediadiversified.org/2018/01/14/on-being-exceptional-the-trap-of-thinking-we-can-do-and-be-diversity-differently/

Almeida, S. (2019). Mythical encounters: Challenging racism in the diverse city. *International Journal of Sociology and Social Policy*, 39(11/12), 937–49. https://doi.org/10.1108/IJSSP-11-2018-0198

Almeida, S. (2021, 14 April). *Decoding diversity speak: How racism thrives through inclusion* [Video]. Transforming social work speaker series 2021, McGill University. YouTube. https://youtu.be/FapQY54L_ZM

Althusser, L. (1971). Ideology and the ideological state apparatuses. In J. Storey (Ed.), *Cultural theory and popular culture: A reader* (pp. 153–64). University of Georgia Press.

Andrews, A. (1992). *Review of race relations practices in the Metropolitan Toronto Police Force*. Metropolitan Audit Department.

Antonsich, M. (2010). Searching for belonging: An analytical framework. *Geography Compass*, 4(6), 644–59. https://doi.org/10.1111/j.1749-8198.2009 .00317.x

Averill, J. (2009). *Diversity matters: Changing the face of public boards*. The Maytree Foundation. https://maytree.com/wp-content/uploads/DiversityMatters .pdf

Back, L., Keith, M., Khan, A., Shukra, K., & Solomos, J. (2009). Islam and the new political landscape. *Theory, Culture & Society*, 26(4), 1–23. https://doi .org/10.1177/0263276409104965

Bannerji, H. (1997). Geography lessons: On being an insider/outsider to the Canadian nation. In L. Roman & L. Eyre (Eds.), *Dangerous territories: Struggles for difference and equality* (pp. 23–41). Routledge.

Bannerji, H. (2000). The paradox of diversity: The construction of a multicultural Canada and "women of color." *Women's Studies International Forum*, 23(5), 537–60. https://doi.org/10.1016/S0277-5395(00)00130-8

Barton, L., & Almeida, S. (2020, 29 November). *White supremacy and the exception to the rule* [Video]. The Dr. Vibe Show. YouTube. https://youtu .be/13G2gJFJ_qc

Bateman, C. (2014, 12 December). The grim history of the Ku Klux Klan in Toronto. *Spacing Magazine*. http://spacing.ca/toronto/2014/12/12/grim -history-ku-klux-klan-toronto/

Beattie, S. (2017, 22 November). Toronto city staff ask for $1 million to confront anti-Black racism. *Toronto Star*. https://www.thestar.com/news/city _hall/2017/11/21/toronto-city-staff-ask-for-1-million-to-confront-anti -black-racism.html

Bhabha, H.K. (1994). *The location of culture*. Routledge.

Bhavnani, R., Mirza, H.S., & Meetoo, V. (2005). *Tackling the roots of racism: Lessons for success*. Policy Press.

Bilge, S. (2013). Intersectionality undone. *Du Bois Review: Social Science Research on Race*, 10(2), 405–24. https://doi.org/10.1017/S1742058X13000283

Bogart, N. (2019, 27 November). *Encyclopedia of hate: A look at the neo-Nazi militant movements with roots in Canada.* CTV News. https://www.ctvnews.ca/canada/encyclopedia-of-hate-a-look-at-the-neo-nazi-militant-movements-with-roots-in-canada-1.4704470

Boudreau, J., Keil, R., & Young, D. (2009). *Changing Toronto: Governing urban neoliberalism.* University of Toronto Press.

Brown, W. (2019). *In the ruins of neoliberalism: The rise of antidemocratic politics in the west.* Columbia University Press.

Bowden, B. (2017, 19 September). Contentious signs jettisoned in north Arkansas city; one called diversity "code word for white genocide." *Arkansas Democrat Gazette.* https://www.arkansasonline.com/news/2017/sep/19/contentious-harrison-signs-are-jettison/

Bryman, A. (2001). *Social research methods.* Oxford University Press.

Butler, J. (1990). *Gender trouble: Feminism and the subversion of identity.* Routledge.

Butler, J. (1997). *The psychic life of power: Theories in subjection.* Stanford University Press.

Butler, J. (2011). *Bodies that matter: On the discursive limits of sex.* Routledge.

Caldwell, R. (2007). Agency and change: Re-evaluating Foucault's legacy. *Organization, 14*(6), 769–91. https://doi.org/10.1177/1350508407082262

Came, H. (2014). Sites of institutional racism in public health policy making in New Zealand. *Social Science & Medicine, 106,* 214–20. https://doi.org/10.1016/j.socscimed.2014.01.055

Carrillo Rowe, A. (2005). Be-longing: Toward a feminist politics of relation. *NWSA Journal, 17*(2), 15–37. https://doi.org/10.1215/9780822389200-002

Catungal, J.P., & Leslie, D. (2009). Contesting the creative city: Race, nation, multiculturalism. *Geoforum, 40*(5), 701–4. https://doi.org/10.1016/j.geoforum.2009.05.005

CBC News. (2016, 18 April). *Black Lives Matter has "absolutely rejected" private meeting but offer stands, Mayor Tory says.* CBC News. https://www.cbc.ca/news/canada/toronto/toronto-mayor-john-tory-addresses-media-1.3541067

Cheng, A.A. (2001). *The melancholy of race: Psychoanalysis, assimilation, and hidden grief.* Oxford University Press.

City of Toronto. (n.d.-a). *2015–2018 City of Toronto strategic plan.* https://www.toronto.ca/wp-content/uploads/2018/01/8d03-Equity-Diversity-Plan-2015-2018.pdf

City of Toronto. (n.d.-b) *Toronto City Council and committees meetings, agendas and minutes.* http://app.toronto.ca/tmmis/findAgendaItem.do?function=doPrepare

City of Toronto. (1953–94). *Reference copies of Metropolitan Toronto committee minutes* (Fonds 220, Series 1889). City of Toronto Archives, Toronto, ON, Canada. https://gencat.eloquent-systems.com/city-of-toronto-archives-m-permalink.html?key=467508

City of Toronto. (1980a, 23 July). *Appendix "A"* (City of Toronto Executive Committee Report No. 37).

City of Toronto. (1980b, 2 October). *The minutes of the council.*

City of Toronto. (1981a, 20 January). *Appendix "A"* (City of Toronto Executive Committee Report No. 7).

City of Toronto. (1981b, 27 July). *Appendix "A"* (City of Toronto Executive Committee Report No. 42).

City of Toronto. (1989a). Executive Committee Report (No. 4).

City of Toronto. (1989b). *1989 Reports adopted by Toronto City Council* (City Council Executive Committee Report No. 1).

City of Toronto. (1990a). *1990 reports adopted by Toronto City Council* (City Council Board of Health Report No. 5, 7.1289).

City of Toronto. (1990b). *1990 reports adopted by Toronto City Council* (City of Toronto Executive Committee Report No. 20).

City of Toronto. (1991a, 15 January). City of Toronto Executive Committee report no. 1 for City Council consideration at meeting no. 2.

City of Toronto. (1991b). City of Toronto Executive Committee report no. 9 for City Council consideration at meeting no. 8.

City of Toronto. (1991c). City of Toronto Neighbourhoods Committee report no. 6 for City Council consideration at meeting no. 8.

City of Toronto. (1992a, 23 March). City of Toronto Executive Committee report no. 9 for City Council consideration at meeting no. 6.

City of Toronto (1992b, 13 April). City of Toronto Executive Committee report no. 13 for City Council Consideration at meeting no. 7.

City of Toronto. (1992c, 7 December). *Minutes of Toronto City Council, additional business communication, 22.*

City of Toronto. (1993a, 13 April). City of Toronto Neighbourhoods Committee report no. 5 for City Council consideration at meeting no. 6.

City of Toronto. (1993b, 30 August). City of Toronto Neighbourhoods Committee report no. 10 for City Council consideration at meeting no. 11.

City of Toronto. (1994, 9 May). City of Toronto Executive Committee report no. 14 for City Council consideration at meeting no. 7.

City of Toronto. (1998a, 28 October). Clause no. 4 of report no. 21 of the strategic policies and priorities committee headed "Coat of Arms for the City of Toronto." In *Minutes of the Council of the City of Toronto* (p. 1813). https://www.toronto.ca/legdocs/1998/minutes/council/cc981028.pdf

City of Toronto. (1998b). *Terms of reference for the City of Toronto: Task force on community access and equity.* https://www.toronto.ca/legdocs/1998/agendas/council/cc/cc980304/tr3rpt/cl006.htm

City of Toronto. (1999a). *Final report: Task force on community access and equity.* https://www.toronto.ca/legdocs/1999/agendas/council/cc/cc990202/sp2rpt/cl006.htm

City of Toronto. (1999b). *Framework for citizen participation in the City of Toronto.* https://www.toronto.ca/legdocs/1999/agendas/council/cc/cc990302/tr2rpt/cl002.htm

City of Toronto. (1999c). *Resources for access and equity functions and final recommendations of the task force on community access and equity.* https://www.toronto.ca/legdocs/1999/agendas/council/cc/cc990609/sp10rpt/cl002.htm

City of Toronto. (1999d). *Toronto Police Association poster and stereotyping of the Hispanic community.* https://www.toronto.ca/legdocs/1999/agendas/council/cc/cc990706/adm1rpt/cl002.htm

City of Toronto. (2000a). *Allocations: 2000 access and equity grant program.* https://www.toronto.ca/legdocs/2000/agendas/council/cc/cc000704/adm14rpt/cl017.pdf

City of Toronto. (2000b). *Certificate of amendments: Notices of motion appearing under item P "no. 15: Establishment of a diversity advocate position."* https://www.toronto.ca/legdocs/2000/agendas/council/cc/cc001205/cofa.pdf

City of Toronto. (2001a). *Development of a City of Toronto declaration and plan of action regarding the elimination of racism in relation to the United Nations: World Conference against Racism, Racial Discrimination, Xenophobia and Related Intolerance (UN-WCAR).* https://www.toronto.ca/legdocs/2001/agendas/council/cc010424/pof4rpt/cl009.pdf

City of Toronto. (2001b). *Diversity advocate action plan.* https://www.toronto.ca/legdocs/2001/agendas/council/cc010306/pof2rpt/cl004.pdf

City of Toronto. (2001c). *2001 access and equity grant program allocations.* https://www.toronto.ca/legdocs/2001/agendas/council/cc010626/adm10rpt/cl002.pdf

City of Toronto. (2002a). *(5) Vandalism of the Gayatri Mandir.* In *Certificate of amendments* (p. 31). https://www.toronto.ca/legdocs/2002/agendas/council/cc020304/cofa.pdf

City of Toronto. (2002b). *Increasing Toronto's profile internationally and at home (all wards).* https://www.toronto.ca/legdocs/2002/agendas/council/cc021126/edp10rpt/cl001.pdf

City of Toronto. (2002c). *International policy framework for the City of Toronto.* https://www.toronto.ca/legdocs/2002/agendas/council/cc020521/pof8rpt/cl009.pdf

City of Toronto. (2002d). *Notice of motion: Principle of zero tolerance of racial profiling for policing in the City of Toronto.* https://www.toronto.ca/legdocs/2002/agendas/council/cc021029/nomj%289%29.pdf

City of Toronto. (2002e). *Notice of motion: Request to federal government to petition the government of Nigeria regarding Amina Lawal law.* https://www.toronto.ca/legdocs/2002/agendas/council/cc021001/nomj%289%29.pdf

City of Toronto. (2002f). *Re: CAO's status report: Implementation of the recommendations of the final report of the task force on community access and equity.* https://www.toronto.ca/legdocs/2002/agendas/committees/pof/pof021114/it009a.pdf

City of Toronto. (2002g). *Update on Toronto response for youth (TRY).* https://www.toronto.ca/legdocs/2002/agendas/committees/cms/cms020624/it015.pdf

City of Toronto. (2003a). *City of Toronto plan of action for the elimination of racism and discrimination.* https://www.toronto.ca/legdocs/2003/agendas/council/cc030414/pof3rpt/cl003.pdf

City of Toronto. (2003b). *Update: Council motion on racial profiling in Toronto.* https://www.toronto.ca/legdocs/2003/agendas/council/cc030204/pof1rpt/cl016.pdf

City of Toronto. (2004). *"If low income women of colour counted in Toronto" report: Implications for parks and recreation.* https://www.toronto.ca/legdocs/2004/agendas/committees/edp/edp041122/it002.pdf

City of Toronto. (2006). *Pilot project: Implementation of an equity lens and equity impact statement.* https://www.toronto.ca/legdocs/2006/agendas/council/cc060925/pof7rpt/cl004.pdf

City of Toronto. (1998–2008). *Toronto City Council of Committee meeting, agenda and minutes: Legacy search.* http://www.toronto.ca/legdocs/legacy-search.htm

City of Toronto. (2009a). *Diversity and positive workplace strategy.* https://www.toronto.ca/legdocs/mmis/2009/el/bgrd/backgroundfile-25339.pdf

City of Toronto. (2009b). *Toronto Police Services Board: Aboriginal policing – statement of commitment and guiding principles.* https://www.toronto.ca/legdocs/mmis/2009/ex/bgrd/backgroundfile-19994.pdf

City of Toronto. (2010). Request for an apology for the media article "Too Asian?" by Councillor Mike Layton seconded by Councillor Kristyn Wong-Tam. https://www.toronto.ca/legdocs/mmis/2011/mm/bgrd/backgroundfile-34300.pdf

City of Toronto. (2012a). *Recreation service plan 2013–2017.* https://www.toronto.ca/legdocs/mmis/2012/cd/bgrd/backgroundfile-51832.pdf

City of Toronto. (2012b). *Supplementary report: 2011 progress report on equity, diversity and human rights achievements.* https://www.toronto.ca/legdocs/mmis/2012/ex/bgrd/backgroundfile-48053.pdf

City of Toronto. (2013). *Notice of motion: Reaffirming Toronto's strong support for freedom of religion and expression, by Councillor James Pasternak, seconded by Councillor Joe Mihevc.* https://www.toronto.ca/legdocs/mmis/2013/mm/bgrd/backgroundfile-62165.pdf

City of Toronto. (2014a). *Aboriginal employment strategy.* https://www.toronto.ca/legdocs/mmis/2014/ex/bgrd/backgroundfile-66236.pdf

City of Toronto. (2014b). *Deputy mayor's Black business professionals roundtable.* https://www.toronto.ca/legdocs/mmis/2014/ed/bgrd/backgroundfile-72675.pdf

City of Toronto. (2014c). *Improving the equity impact statement.* https://www.toronto.ca/legdocs/mmis/2014/ex/bgrd/backgroundfile-69450.pdf

City of Toronto. (2017a). *Affirming council support for the Toronto Police Service.* https://www.toronto.ca/legdocs/mmis/2017/ex/bgrd/backgroundfile-105821.pdf

City of Toronto. (2017b). *The interim Toronto action plan to confront anti-Black racism.*

City of Toronto. (2017c). *TO prosperity: Toronto poverty reduction strategy 2017 report and 2018 work plan.* https://www.toronto.ca/legdocs/mmis/2017/ex/bgrd/backgroundfile-109105.pdf

City of Toronto. (2017d). *Attachment B: Poverty reduction strategy 2018 work plan.* https://www.toronto.ca/legdocs/mmis/2017/ex/bgrd/backgroundfile-109110.pdf

City of Toronto. (2017e). *Toronto action plan to confront anti-Black racism.* https://www.toronto.ca/legdocs/mmis/2017/ex/bgrd/backgroundfile-109127.pdf

Cole, D. (2015, 21 April). The skin I'm in: I've been interrogated by police more than 50 times – all because I'm Black. *Toronto Life.* https://torontolife.com/life/skin-im-ive-interrogated-police-50-times-im-black/

Coleman, D. (2015). Afterword: A two row ethics of encounter. In C. Janzen, D. Jeffery, & K. Smith (Eds.), *Unravelling encounters: Ethics, knowledge, and resistance under neoliberalism* (chap. 12). Wilfred Laurier University Press.

Cowen, D., & Parlette, V. (2011). *Toronto's inner suburbs: Investing in social infrastructure in Scarborough.* University of Toronto Press.

Croucher, S.L. (1997). Constructing the image of ethnic harmony in Toronto Canada: The politics of problem definition and nondefinition. *Urban Affairs Review, 32*(3), 319–47. https://doi.org/10.1177/107808749703200302

Darder, A., & Torres, R. (2004). *After race: Racism after multiculturalism.* New York University Press.

Davies, B. (1991). The concept of agency: A feminist poststructuralist analysis. *Social Analysis, 30,* 42–53.

Davies, B. (2000). *A body of writing: 1990–1999.* Altamira Press.

Dhaliwal, A.K. (1996). Can the subaltern vote? Radical democracy and questions of race. In D. Trend (Ed.), *Radical democracy: Identity, citizenship, and the state* (pp. 42–61). Routledge.

Emerson, R.M., Fretz, R.I., & Shaw, L.L. (1995). Processing fieldnotes: Coding and memoing. *Writing ethnographic fieldnotes* (chap. 6). The University of Chicago Press.

Fairclough, N. (1993). Critical discourse analysis and the marketization of public discourse: The universities. *Discourse & Society, 4*(2), 133–68. https://doi.org/10.1177/0957926593004002002

Fakier, K. (2018). Women and renewable energy in a South African community: Exploring energy poverty and environmental racism. *Journal of International Women's Studies, 19*(5), 165–76.

Fanon, F. (1952). *Black skin, white masks: A new edition translated from the French by Richard Philcox.* Grove Press.

Fanon, F. (1967). *Black skin, white masks* (C. Lam Markmann, Trans.). Grove Press.

Farley, A. (1997). The Black body as fetish object. *Oregon Law Review, 76,* 457–535.

Ferreira da Silva, D. (2007). *Toward a global idea of race.* The University of Minnesota Press.

Ferreira da Silva, D. (2014). No-bodies: Law, raciality and violence. *Meritum – Belo Horizonte, 9*(1), 119–62.

Ferreira da Silva, D. (2015). Before man: Sylvia Wynter's rewriting of the modern episteme. In K. McKittrick (Ed.), *Sylvia Wynter: On being human as praxis* (pp. 90–105). Duke University Press.

Foucault, M. (1970). *The order of things: An archaeology of the human sciences.* Tavistock.

Foucault, M. (1979). Governmentality. *Ideology and Consciousness, 6,* 5–21.

Foucault, M. (1980). Two lectures. In C. Gordon (Ed.), *Power/Knowledge: Selected interviews and other writings 1972–1977* (pp. 78–108). Pantheon.

Foucault, M. (1981). The order of discourse. In R. Young (Ed.), *Untying the text: A post-structuralist reader* (pp. 57–78). Routledge & Kegan Paul.

Foucault, M. (1984). Nietzsche, genealogy, history. In P. Rabinow (Ed.), *The Foucault reader* (pp. 76–100). Random House.

Foucault, M. (1991). Questions of method. In G. Burchell, C. Gordon, & P. Miller (Eds.), *The Foucault effect: Studies in governmentality* (pp. 73–86). Harvester Wheatsheaf.

Frisken, F. (1991). The contributions of metropolitan government to the success of Toronto's public transit system: An empirical dissent from the public-choice paradigm. *Urban Affairs Quarterly, 27*(2), 268–92. https://doi.org/10.1177/004208169102700208

Goldberg, D.T. (1993). *Racist culture: Philosophy and the politics of meaning.* Blackwell Publishers.

Goldberg, D.T. (2002). *The racial state.* Blackwell Publishers.

Goldberg, D.T. (2009). *The threat of race: Reflections on racial neoliberalism.* Blackwell Publishing.

Good, K.R. (2009). *Municipalities and multiculturalism: The politics of immigration in Toronto and Vancouver.* University of Toronto Press.

Goonewardena, K., & Kipfer, S. (2005). Spaces of difference: Reflections from Toronto on multiculturalism, bourgeois urbanism and the possibility of radical urban politics. *International Journal of Urban and Regional Research, 29*(3), 670–8. https://doi.org/10.1111/j.1468-2427.2005.00611.x

Graham, K.A., & Phillips, S.D. (2007). Another fine balance: Managing diversity in Canadian cities. In K.G. Banting, T.J. Courchene, & F.L. Seidle (Eds.), *The art of the state III: Belonging? Diversity, recognition and shared citizenship in Canada* (pp. 155–94). Institute for Research on Public Policy (IRPP).

Gramlich, J. (2020, 26 October). *What the 2020 electorate looks like by party, race and ethnicity, age, education and religion*. Pew Research Center. https://www.pewresearch.org/fact-tank/2020/10/26/what-the-2020-electorate-looks-like-by-party-race-and-ethnicity-age-education-and-religion/

Green, J. (2017). The impossibility of citizenship liberation for Indigenous people. In J. Mann (Ed.), *Citizenship in transnational perspective* (pp. 175–88). Palgrave Macmillan. https://doi.org/10.1007/978-3-319-53529-6_9

Gross, J.S. (2007). Diversity and the democratic challenge: Governing world cities. In R. Hambleton, & J.S. Gross (Eds.), *Governing cities in a global era: Urban innovation, competition, and democratic reform* (pp. 73–91). Palgrave Macmillan.

Hall, S. (1988). *The hard road to renewal: Thatcherism and the crisis of the left.* Verso.

Hall, S. (1996). Cultural identity and diaspora. In P. Mongia (Ed.), *Contemporary postcolonial theory: A reader* (pp. 110–21). Arnold.

Hall, S. (1997). *Representation: Cultural representations and signifying practices.* Sage Publications.

Hall, S. (2017). The neoliberal revolution 2011. In S. Davison, D. Featherstone, M. Rustin, & B. Schwarz (Eds.), *Selected political writings: The great moving right show and other essays* (pp. 317–35). Duke University Press.

Hall, S. (2021). Teaching race. In P. Gilroy & R. Wilson Gilmore (Eds.), *Selected writings on race and difference* (pp. 123–35). Duke University Press.

Henry, F., Dua, E., James, C.E., Kobayashi, A., Li, P., Ramos, H., & Smith, M.S. (2017). *The equity myth: Racialization and indigeneity at Canadian universities.* UBC Press.

Hook, D. (2001). Discourse, knowledge, materiality: Foucault and discourse analysis. *Theory and Psychology, 11*(4), 521–47. https://doi.org/10.1177/0959354301114006

Hook, D. (2005). The racial stereotype, colonial discourse, fetishism, and racism. *Psychoanalytic Review, 92*(5), 701–34. https://doi.org/10.1521/prev.2005.92.5.701

Hook, D. (2006). "Pre-discursive" racism. *Journal of Community and Applied Social Psychology, 16*(3), 207–32. https://doi.org/10.1002/casp.853

Hook, D. (2007). *Foucault, psychology and the analytics of power.* Palgrave Macmillan.

Hook, D. (2011). Psychoanalytic contributions to the political analysis of affect and identification. *Ethnicities, 11*(1), 107–15. https://doi.org/10.1177/1468796810388703

hooks, b. (1992). *Black looks: Race and representation*. South End Press.

Jackson, P. (1994). Constructions of criminality: Police-community relations in Toronto. *Antipode, 26*(3), 216–35.

Jacobs, J. (1996). *The edge of empire: Postcolonialism and the city*. Routledge.

Jordan, G., & Weedon, C. (2015). The celebration of difference and the cultural politics of racism. In B. Adam & S. Allan (Eds.), *Theorizing culture: An interdisciplinary critique after postmodernism* (pp. 149–64). Routledge.

Joseph, A.J., Janes, J., Badwall, H., & Almeida, S. (2019). Preserving white comfort and safety: The politics of race erasure in academe. *Social Identities, 26*(2), 166–85. https://doi.org/10.1080/13504630.2019.1671184

Joy, M., & Vogel, R.K. (2015). Toronto's governance crisis: A global city under pressure. *Cities, 49*, 35–52. https://doi.org/10.1016/j.cities.2015.06.009

Keil, R. (2002). "Common-sense" neoliberalism: Progressive conservative urbanism in Toronto, Canada. *Antipode, 34*(3), 578–601. https://doi.org/10.1002/9781444397499.ch10

Keil, R., & Kipfer, S. (2003). The urban experience and globalization. In W. Clement & L.F. Vosko (Eds.), *Changing Canada: Political economy as transformation* (pp. 335–62). McGill-Queen's University Press.

Khosla, P. (2003). *If low income women counted in Toronto: Final report of the action-research project "Breaking isolation, getting involved."* The Community Social Planning Council of Toronto. https://www.oaith.ca/assets/files/Publications/Low_Income_Women_of_Colour.pdf

Kristeva, J. (1982). *Powers of horror: An essay on abjection* (L.S. Roudiez, Trans.). Columbia University Press.

Kymlicka, W. (1995). *Multicultural citizenship: A liberal theory of minority rights*. Oxford University Press.

Ladson-Billings, G. (2000). Racialized discourses and ethnic epistemologies. In N.K. Denzin & Y.S. Lincoln (Eds.), *Handbook of qualitative research* (2nd ed., pp. 257–77). Sage Publications.

Lee, S.-I. (2008). Recognition as a depleted source in Lynne Tillman's motion sickness. In R.M. Berry & J.R. Di Leo (Eds.), *Fiction's present: Situating contemporary narrative innovation* (pp. 195–208). State University of New York Press.

Lentin, A. (2011). *Contemporary issues: Racism and ethnic discrimination*. The Rosen Publishing Group.

Lentin, A., & Titley, G. (2011). *The crisis of multiculturalism: Racism in a neoliberal age*. Zed Books.

Lorde, A. (1984). *Sister outsider: Essays and speeches*. Crossing Press.

Lowe, L. (2015). *The intimacies of four continents*. Duke University Press.

Makinde, O. (2019). *Towards a health city: Addressing anti-Black racism in Vancouver*. City of Vancouver and University of British Columbia. https://sustain.ubc.ca/sites/default/files/2019-68_Towards%20a%20Healthy%20City%20-%20Addressing_Makinde.pdf

Mascarenhas, M. (2012). *Where the waters divide: Neoliberalism, white privilege, and environmental racism in Canada*. Lexington Books.

Matus, C., & Infante, M. (2011). Undoing diversity: Knowledge and neoliberal discourses in colleges of education. *Discourse: Studies in the Cultural Politics of Education, 32*(3), 293–307. https://doi.org/10.1080/01596306.2011.573248

Mayo, C. (2002). The binds that tie: Civility and social difference. *Educational Theory, 52*(2), 169–86. https://doi.org/10.1111/j.1741-5446.2002.00169.x

McDonald, C., & Davey, E. (Hosts). (2016, 6 May). More or less: The world's most diverse city [Audio podcasts]. In *More or Less: Behind the Stats*. BBC Radio 4. https://www.bbc.co.uk/programmes/p03v1r1p

Mele, C. (2019). The strategic uses of race to legitimize "social mix" urban redevelopment. *Social Identities, 25*(3), 27–40. https://doi.org/10.1080/13504630.2017.1418603

Miles, M.B., & Huberman, A.M. (1994). *Qualitative data analysis: An expanded sourcebook* (2nd ed.). Sage Publications.

Mills, C.W. (1997). *The racial contract*. Cornell University Press.

Mohanram, R. (1999). *Black body: Women, colonialism, and space*. University of Minnesota Press.

Municipality of Metropolitan Toronto. (1977). *Walter Pitman report: Now is not too late*.

Municipality of Metropolitan Toronto (1978). Appendix "A": Report of Committee to Consider Report of Task Force on Human Relations, June 13. In *Municipality of Metropolitan Toronto report no. 1 of the special committee to consider the report of the task force on human relations*.

Nasser, S. (2017, 13 May). *City unveils draft action plan to combat anti-Black racism, asks "Did we get it right?"* CBC News. https://www.cbc.ca/news/canada/toronto/antiblack-racism-action-plan-toronto-1.4114355

NOW Staff. (2018, 14 August). Of "thugs." "gangsters" and "sewer rats" why John Tory's language on gun violence is a problem. *Now Toronto*. https://nowtoronto.com/news/john-tory-gun-violence-racism

Okolie, A.C. (2005). Toward an anti-racist research framework: The case for interventive in-depth interviewing. In G.J.S. Dei & G.S. Johal (Eds.), *Critical issues in anti-racist research methodologies* (pp. 242–68). Peter Lang Publishing.

Ontario Human Rights Commission. (2010). *Antiracism and antidiscrimination for municipalities: Introductory manual*. https://www.ohrc.on.ca/en/anti-racism-and-anti-discrimination-municipalities-introductory-manual

Parker, J. (2012). Questioning appropriation: Agency and complicity in a transnational feminist location politics. *Journal of Feminist Scholarship, 3*, 1–18.

Paschel, T.S. (2016). *Becoming Black political subjects: Movements and ethno-racial rights in Colombia and Brazil*. Princeton University Press.

Poisson, A. (2018, 11 January). Practicing intersectionality: Against the colonization of Black thought in white feminist discourse. *Medium.* https://medium.com/@arianepoisson/practicing-intersectionality-against-the-colonization-of-black-thought-in-white-feminist-discourse-fa4db9ef96b8

Probyn, E. (1996). *Outside belonging.* Routledge.

Puwar, N. (2001). The racialised somatic norm and the senior civil service. *Sociology, 35*(3), 651–70. https://doi.org/10.1177/S0038038501000335

Puwar, N. (2004). *Space invaders: Race, gender and bodies out of place.* Berg Publishers.

Qadeer, M.A. (2016). *Multicultural cities: Toronto, New York, and Los Angeles.* University of Toronto Press.

Razack, S.H. (2002). Introduction: When place becomes race. In S.H. Razack (Ed.), *Race, space and the law: Unmapping a white settler society* (pp. 1–20). Between the Lines.

Razack, S.H. (2007). Stealing the pain of others: Reflections on Canadian humanitarian responses. *Review of Education, Pedagogy, and Cultural Studies, 29*(4), 375–94. https://doi.org/10.1080/10714410701454198

Roach, K. (1999). *Due process and victims' rights: The new law and politics of criminal justice.* University of Toronto Press.

Rosa, V. (2019). Interrogating multiculturalism and urban revitalization: "The diversity of diversity" in Toronto's Regent Park. *Journal of Critical Race Inquiry, 6*(1), 32–61.

Rose, N. (1996). Identity, genealogy, history. In S. Hall & P. Du Gay (Eds.), *Questions of cultural identity* (pp. 128–50). SAGE Publications.

Rose, N., O'Malley, P., & Valverde, M. (2009). Governmentality. *Annual Review of Law and Social Science, 2*, 83–104.

Said, E.W. (1979). *Orientalism.* Vintage Books.

Saloojee, A. (2003). *Social inclusion, anti-racism and democratic citizenship.* Laidlaw Foundation. https://laidlawfdn.org/assets/wpsosi_2003_jan_social-inclusion-anti-racism.pdf

Schulman, S. (2021). *Let the record show: A political history of Act Up New York, 1987–1993.* Farrar, Straus and Giroux.

Shaw, W.S. (2007). *Cities of whiteness.* Blackwell Publishing.

Siemiatycki, M. (2011). Governing immigrant city: Immigrant political representation in Toronto. *American Behavioral Scientist, 55*(9), 1214–34. https://doi.org/10.1177/0002764211407840

Skrbiš, Z., Baldassar, L., & Poynting, S. (2007). Introduction – Negotiating belonging: Migration and generations. *Journal of Intercultural Studies, 28*(3), 261–9. https://doi.org/10.1080/07256860701429691

Smith, D.E. (1999). *Writing the social: Critique, theory, and investigations.* University of Toronto Press.

Smith, M.S. (2010). Gender, whiteness and "other Others" in the academy. In S. Razack, S. Thobani, & M. Smith (Eds.), *States of race: Critical race feminism for the 21st century* (pp. 37–58). Between the Lines.

Stoler, A.L. (1995). *Race and the education of desire: Foucault's history of sexuality and the colonial order of things.* Duke University Press.

Tamboukou, M. (1999). Writing genealogies: An exploration of Foucault's strategies for doing research. *Discourse: Studies in the Cultural Politics of Education, 20*(2), 201–17. https://doi.org/10.1080/0159630990200202

Tasan-Kok, T., & Ozogul, S. (2017). *DIVERCITIES, living with urban diversity: The case of Toronto.* University of Amsterdam and TU Delft, Amsterdam and Delft.

Thobani, S. (2007). *Exalted subjects: Studies in the making of race and nation in Canada.* University of Toronto Press.

Tossutti, L.S. (2012). Municipal roles in immigrant settlement, integration and cultural diversity. *Canadian Journal of Political Science, 45*(3), 607–33. https://doi.org/10.1017/S000842391200073X

Trinh, M. (1989). *Woman, native, other.* University of Indiana Press.

Tuck, E. (2009). Suspending damage: A letter to communities. *Harvard Educational Review, 79*(3), 409–27. https://doi.org/10.17763/haer.79.3.n0016675661t3n15

Valverde, M. (2012). *Everyday law on the street: City governance in an age of diversity.* University of Chicago Press.

van Dijk, T.A. (2002). Discourse and racism. In D.T. Goldberg & J. Solomos (Eds.), *A companion to racial and ethnic studies* (pp. 145–59). Blackwell Publishing.

Weedon, C. (1997). *Feminist practice and poststructuralist theory* (2nd ed.). Blackwell Publishing.

Weedon, C. (2004). *Identity and culture: Narratives of difference and belonging.* Open University Press.

Yuval-Davis, N. (2007). Intersectionality, citizenship and contemporary politics of belonging. *Critical Review of International Social and Political Philosophy, 10*(4), 561–74. https://doi.org/10.1080/13698230701660220

Zhou, S. (2018, 21 November). White nationalist posts photos of racially diverse Toronto school children to "prove" white genocide. *Vice.* https://www.vice.com/en_ca/article/7xyxwd/white-nationalist-posts-photos-of-racially-diverse-school-children-to-prove-white-genocide

Zhuang, Z. (2018). Toronto: Planning for diversity, inclusion and urban resilience. *Cities of Migration.* https://doi.org/10.32920/ryerson.14640003.v1

Index